100
OUR SENSES GAMES
0 TO 3

C000225806

Easy-to-play games

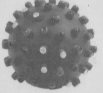

Supporting first learning

Stages of development

ALICE SHARP

CREDITS

British Library Cataloguing-in-Publication Data A catalogue record for this book is available from the British Library.

ISBN 0 439 97129 2

The right of Alice Sharp to be identified as the author of this work has been asserted by her in accordance with the Copyright, Designs and Patents Act 1988.

All rights reserved. This book is sold subject to the condition that it shall not, by way of trade or otherwise, be lent, hired out or otherwise circulated without the publisher's prior consent in any form of binding or cover other than that in which it is published and without a similar condition, including this condition, being imposed upon the subsequent purchaser.

No part of this publication may be reproduced, stored in a retrieval system, or transmitted, in any form or by any means, electronic, mechanical, photocopying, recording or otherwise, without the prior permission of the publisher. This book remains copyright, although permission is granted to copy pages where indicated for classroom distribution and use only in the school which has purchased the book, or by the teacher who has purchased the book, and in accordance with the CLA licensing agreement. Photocopying permission is given only for purchasers and not for borrowers of books from any lending service.

Author
Alice Sharp

Illustrations
Gaynor Berry

Editor
Sally Gray

Assistant Editor
Kate Element

Series Designer
Anna Oliwa

Designer
Andrea Lewis

Text © 2004 Alice Sharp
© 2004 Scholastic Ltd

Designed using Adobe PageMaker

Published by Scholastic Ltd
Villiers House
Clarendon Avenue
Leamington Spa
Warwickshire CV32 5PR

Visit our website at www.scholastic.co.uk
Printed by Belmont Press
1 2 3 4 5 6 7 8 9 0   4 5 6 7 8 9 0 1 2 3

Acknowledgements

The publishers gratefully acknowledge permission to reproduce the following copyright material:

With thanks to the children and staff of Jigsaw Day Nursery, Leamington Spa.

© **Derek Cooknell:** p5, p9, p10, p12, p13, p14, p15, p16, p19, p22, p24, p25, p26, p31, p32, p37, p38, p39, p42, p43, p46, p47, p48, p49, p52b, p57, p58, p60, p62, p65, p67, p68, p71, p72, p75, p79, p81, p83, p84a, p85, p86, p95, p97, p98, p100, p108, p111, p112a, p114, p115, p118, p121.

© **Corbis:** Cover, p7, p112b.

© **Ingram Publishing:** Cover, p3c, p3d, p4a, p4b, p4c, p4d.

© **Photodisc:** Cover, p3a.

© **Dan Powell/SODA:** p52a.

© **Stockbyte:** Cover, p6, p8, p23, p51 ,p83, 84b.

Every effort has been made to trace copyright holders and the publishers apologise for any inadvertent omissions.

CONTENTS

CHAPTER 1

CHAPTER 2

CHAPTER 3

CHAPTER 4

CONTENTS

CHAPTER 5

CHAPTER 6

CHAPTER 7

CHAPTER 8

INTRODUCTION

Your baby's needs

Warmth, comfort and nourishment are the most obvious and immediate needs of a newborn baby. Through your love and concern these needs will be met – it is this love and care that also forms an important part of your baby's long-term development and happiness.

Almost instantly your baby will seek to communicate with you – she will look for food – touching, smelling and tasting the scents of your closeness, her food and the environment that she is now a part of. She will respond to the calm quiet tones of your voice and she will use her eyes to attempt to focus her attention.

This immediate use of all her senses lets us know that she has arrived and is eager to become a major part of the world. This instinctive eagerness to explore her world will lead her through the pattern of emotional and cognitive development. This pattern varies from child to child, based on a number of inherited and external influences. As carers we, of course, are seeking to make all our influences as positive as possible!

Learning through play

The activities in this book place a strong emphasis on play and having fun with your child. In the early years of your child's life, the way she learns to play and the kind of environment that she plays in will contribute enormously to her emotional and cognitive development. When children play, they learn; while they learn, they develop skills; while they learn and develop skills, they should have fun! Sharing 'play' time with your young child should be a time to have fun together – the games in this book will provide you with a wide range of starting points. Each game has a suggested age range, showing whether it will be appropriate for your child. The introductory section at the beginning of each chapter also gives lots of helpful information with regards to stages of development.

The right kind of environment

Most play opportunities for under-threes are best set up on the floor. This means that things don't fall or get spilled, the toys can be spread out over a large area and your young child can approach her 'play space' from any angle. Don't offer too many toys in the 'play space'. Choice is important but too much can be confusing.

Your child will be interested in and want a variety of play activities and materials – some that help to strengthen her body muscles and others that appeal to a range of her senses. Make sure that you provide activities that involve her in balancing, climbing, throwing, pushing and pulling, as well as tasting, touching, smelling, listening and observing. Young children have an endless need to explore, which means that you will always need to ensure that their environment is safe – remain close at hand and watch carefully at all times.

Daily routines and experiences

Strong attachments form when you are available to your child and are sensitive to her needs. As you respond to your child's wants and needs you are showing her how much you enjoy being with her. This tells your child that her needs will be met and leads to a sense of security. Consistency and individual attention are important because of the learning that takes place within your child's early relationships.

The close physical bond between you and your child should never become less important. During her infant, primary and secondary years she will continue to need the love and security she feels when sharing close, caring moments with you. She may not always look for it, but she will rarely turn away from it, should it be offered.

Make your regular routines happy times. At changing time use a comfortable area, where you can be physically close, chatting and singing to your child in an enthusiastic way. Eating times should be in an area suitable to your child's age and stage of development. If you are breastfeeding or bottle-feeding, then hold your baby close to you, making eye contact, smiling and gently caressing her cheeks. If she is older, then ensure that you share the experience together, eating a meal or a snack at the same time.

Sleep time routines should always be carried out in a quiet, calm way. Create a sequence of events for this routine to make your child feel secure and enjoy bedtime. Songs, stories, cuddles, baths, milky drinks and so on, can all be established in a regular order before finally saying goodnight.

Babies and young children feel confident in the knowledge that they are familiar with what is going to happen next. Setting routines during the day usually makes for happy children and more relaxed carers!

The five senses
Touch

Touch is one of the nicest senses to share. The touch of people close to your baby can have a hugely calming and reassuring effect on her. Touch is the sense that your child will use to engage with every new item, material, space and person she is introduced to. Many play opportunities in this book will involve your child in using her hands to explore and experiment with. It is the sense that will lead her to investigate and discover new and exciting properties, ways to manipulate and an understanding of texture.

While your young child is manipulating resources her hand-to-eye co-ordination is being stimulated, her thinking skills are being developed and her sense of wonder is being promoted.

Taste

Generally between the ages of four and six months, and with advice from your health visitor or doctor, your baby will be introduced to solid food. Introducing solids to your baby's diet is important to her development, both physically and cognitively. As your baby progresses from lump-free food to lumpy and finger foods, she is also learning about taste, texture, the physical skills of chewing and swallowing as well as developing her hand-to-eye co-ordination skills. Offer a well-balanced diet and allow her the freedom to experiment with feeding techniques and experiences.

Hearing

Everyday life often offers a barrage of sounds. A distracting environment that has a lot of confusing sounds can hinder active listening. Listening is essential for language development, so it is important to create quiet times to talk, to listen and to play. Balance these times with other opportunities to interact in a busy, lively, sound-filled environment.

Your toddler is able to distinguish well between voices and sounds and can recognise simple tunes which are sung repeatedly by a parent or carer. As well as familiar sounds it is important to provide your child with activities which allow her to explore and experiment with new sounds.

A child who is spoken to as often as possible has more vocabulary and sounds available to imitate. The development of speech is hugely aided by listening and responding to adults and siblings.

Sight

Young children look at everything around them. They love to look at bright bold patterns, to watch the washing going round in the machine or simply to watch you cooking the dinner.

Everyday jobs and experiences that we take for granted can be hugely entertaining to young children. Babies explore their world actively with their eyes, so ensure that whenever you see something of interest you call your child's attention to it. Help your child to make the most of her visual skills by ensuring that objects of interest are placed at appropriate levels for her to enjoy. When playing together, use the toys and equipment yourself as she will gain a great deal from watching you. Help her to enjoy looking at simple picture books and draw her attention to fine details on the pages.

Smell

When your baby entered the world, her sense of smell was perhaps more important to her than at any other point in her life. To begin with, due to limited hearing and vision, your baby relies heavily on her sense of smell to recognise you. She uses it to give herself a better understanding of the world as she gathers information about where she is and who she is with.

The sense of smell is connected to the memory. Your child might recognise your perfume, the smell of her bath oil, her favourite snack and flowers in the garden. While introducing opportunities for her to smell a variety of scents, describe them – helping her to identify and relate to them in the future.

Communicating through the senses

Focusing on your child's senses will provide you with many ways to help her to develop effective communication, social and emotional skills. The activities in the chapters in this book will give you many suggestions and starting points. Take the activities in the chapter devoted to touch, for example – by exploring alongside you, your child will be introduced to the language of touch. As she feels something that is rough, smooth, wet or slippery you will be on hand to provide her with the appropriate vocabulary, allowing her to directly relate a word to something she can actually feel.

Don't forget to use your own senses as you share the games and activities with your child. Enjoy watching her grow and develop, listen to her voice and snuggle up close when you play. Have fun and put time aside to focus your attention on your baby or young child. She deserves it and so do you!

LET'S GET BUSY

How often have you heard someone say, 'Oh, is he not walking yet?', or 'My daughter walked at ten months, you know!'. A baby may walk at ten months or may still be crawling at 15 months – both are normal. Children grow, change, mature and develop at different rates, even identical twins will not be exactly the same. Each child is different because each is an individual. They are born different, they have different lives and they'll learn and experience different things.

EARLY DEVELOPMENT

In the first years of life most children will reach a range of physical milestones from lifting their heads, to pulling themselves up and sitting without support. They may begin to crawl or bottom shuffle, they will pull themselves upright, stand and then walk. Each child will reach these points at different rates, within certain normal limits.

There will be a progression in all sorts of other physical capabilities, such as lifting, stretching, pushing and pulling. They may learn to kick or throw a ball, but again, each child is different and will develop these skills when they are ready and able to. These skills are often referred to as gross motor skills.

How you can help
● Encourage your young child to interact and respond to various equipment such as toys, balls, and safe, clean household objects.
● Place interesting toys near him that can be reached easily. Ensure that they are small enough and easy to lift (though not too small as to pose a choking risk).
● Offer him toys that can be manipulated by pushing. Toys with an element of surprise, such as a sound or a pop-up toy will delight him!
● Toys that can be pulled along will encourage him to realise that toys can be used in a variety of ways.

YOUR ROLE
Your role is also crucial as a supporter, helper and facilitator. Always offer praise and support as your child attempts things – do not keep it just for when he achieves. A child who's given love, encouragement and praise will want to learn more.

One of the best ways for your child to learn is to watch you, another adult or sibling. If he sees you 'demonstrate' an activity or toy then he is likely to copy. If he watches and sees the variety of possibilities then he will feel confident to explore and experiment himself.

There is, however a fine balance to achieve and you should try to avoid helping him all the time, so that he can build his own confidence and independence.

EXERCISE

Even the youngest child wants to use his body to move around, to move things towards him, to gather knowledge and to explore his environment. The more opportunities you give him to crawl, walk, run, jump and climb the more his ability to do this will improve. Because he enjoys attempting these skills he will be happy and content and you will probably find, due to the amount of energy he uses, he will sleep better. At the same time you'll be helping his muscle development and general fitness.

FINE MOTOR SKILLS

As well as gross motor skills, the physical development of your child includes the development of muscles which enable movement. These movements can be very small, such as grasping a spoon, picking up a pen or holding onto the handle of a push along toy. They are called fine motor or manipulative skills.

How you can help

● Offer a range of smaller objects (not so small they cause a choking hazard) for him to explore.

● Make an activity out of everyday routine items such as offering him spoons and blunt cooking utensils to explore.

● Offer him a range of items and objects that he can use to post through a hole in a box or into a container.

● Allow him to turn the pages of a book or magazine as you read it.

Think first! Always supervise your young child and never leave him unattended when he is playing.

Sometimes, it is just as important to sit back and watch your child interact with a toy, so that you are aware of how your child plays and what captures his interest and enthusiasm. By all means, support him with your praise and suggestions but during your observations try not to play until he looks for you to become involved.

How you can help

● Sit near to where your child is playing, watch him as he explores the toys and objects you have given him. If he looks for you to be involved, then play with him.

● While he is experimenting, for example with how he can make a noise or move something, offer encouragement and praise.

● Place one or two objects on the floor between you both. Play with one of the items and encourage him to watch. Allow him to play alongside you with the other toy if that is what he prefers.

● Join in while he is using something he is familiar with and demonstrate another way it could be used.

How you can help

● Make time for your child to become involved in experiences that involve exercise. Move his fingers and hands and his arms and legs – perhaps during gentle rough and tumble, or during action rhymes.

● Enjoy little bursts of stretching and walking, bending and turning.

● Allow him to lie, nappy free, kicking and punching the air or something suspended above him, so that he can 'target practice'.

● If he is crawling, clear as much floor space as possible, making sure that the space is safe. Allow him to move around freely.

● Encourage him to walk rather than use the pushchair or be carried around.

● Take him to the park or an area where he can run freely, climb and explore.

AGE RANGE
0-1 year

LEARNING OPPORTUNITIES
● To encourage active reaching and stretching
● To develop attention and concentration
● To visually stimulate and encourage a response.

YOU WILL NEED
An old baby mobile or two dowelling rods and string; some bright fabric swatches; a few sheets of holographic wrapping paper; a few small toys or small boxes of different shapes; brightly-coloured ribbons; sticky tape; scissors.

Up above

Sharing the game
● Remove the small toys from your baby's mobile, or cover them by wrapping a piece of bright fabric over each toy, tying it securely with a stitch or elastic band.
● Alternatively tie the two dowelling rods in a cross shape with some brightly-coloured ribbon.
● Take the objects you have gathered and cover each one in a different fabric or paper. Attach a ribbon to each object and tie them to the ends of the dowelling rods.
● Next, fix a variety of ribbons to the covered toys or boxes and let them dangle freely.

● Use the required length of string to hang the new mobile above the changing mat, bouncy chair or cot.
● While singing to your baby, gently blow the ribbons and encourage her to stretch and catch them.

Taking it further
● Find some close-up photographs of the baby's face and attach them to the strings of the mobile. Position the photographs so that they are face down and can move freely above your baby in her cot, bouncy chair or changing station.
● Decorate some paper plates and suspend them from the mobile, so that your baby can see the patterns or pictures as they move above their cot.

AGE RANGE
0-1 year

LEARNING OPPORTUNITIES
● To develop a sense of movement
● To develop gross motor skills through rolling
● To encourage listening skills.

YOU WILL NEED
A clear space to gently roll together with baby; a soft quilt; blanket or lengths of material; a few pillows.

Roll me over

Sharing the game
● Place the quilt, lengths of material or blanket on the floor. Lie beside your baby and quietly sing while you move him. Sing:
Roll, roll
One, two, three
Roll, roll
Away from me.

Over and over
Away you go
Over and over
To and fro.
● While you sing the words, roll away from your baby and onto your tummy. Then gently roll him towards you. Make sure that you are always gentle and never shake or roll your child vigorously.
● Next, roll him away from you – leaving enough room for you to roll back over next to him.
● Sing the rhyme each time you repeat the movements. After each new roll, tickle your baby under the chin and tickle each cheek.
● Stop immediately if your child does not respond positively to being rolled.

Taking it further
● Sit opposite your baby and roll different objects to and fro as you sing the rhyme. Try a ball, a rolled up pair of socks and a large plastic bottle filled with liquid. Encourage your baby to roll the object back to you each time.
● Stand in front of your baby and encourage him to roll the ball under your legs. Alternatively, roll the various items under a chair while saying the rhyme.

LEARNING OPPORTUNITIES
● To encourage manipulation of materials
● To develop co-ordination
● To develop gross motor skills while kicking.

YOU WILL NEED
A length of strong, bright ribbon; tin foil; greaseproof paper; sheets of fabric softener; a quilt or blanket; scented tissue; stemmed, scented flowers.

High kick

Sharing the game
● Place a quilt or blanket on a clear space on the floor. Fix a line of bright ribbon securely between two chairs, across the quilt at a height safe for your baby to lie under and kick.
● Hang around six strips of tin foil from one point of the ribbon, six strips of greaseproof paper from another point and six sheets of fabric softener from another. Tie some flowers to the ribbon then a few scented tissues.
● Let your baby lie under the length of ribbon and kick or stretch and 'twirl' the hanging materials.
● Sit and shake each material in turn, describe the texture and the sound of each of the different materials to your baby. Call her attention to the way the various items move.

Taking it further
● Sit slightly in front of the hanging materials, stretch and 'pick' a flower or scented tissue and smell the scent. Help your baby to

choose one and encourage her to enjoy the scent.
● Hang up an array of socks filled with fragrant objects, such as pot pourri, cinnamon sticks and herbal teabags. Attach the socks to the bright line of ribbon. Lift or help your baby to stand as they smell the contents of the socks.

LEARNING OPPORTUNITIES
● To encourage muscle development
● To develop hand-to-eye co-ordination
● To develop the sense of touch.

YOU WILL NEED
A selection of different types of ball, such as plastic, wooden and tennis balls. Other objects that can be rolled, such as a rolled-up pair of socks and a scrunched up piece of aluminium foil. A bright tub or basket; cushions and a sofa.

Stretch across

Sharing the game
● Gather the selection of textured balls and objects that can be rolled and place them in a bright tub or basket.
● Let your baby help by placing the items you choose into the basket. Encourage him to explore the different textures and describe them to him as he touches them.

● Sit quite close to, and opposite, the sofa or some cushions. Place your child next to you.
● Choose one of the balls or objects and roll it to the middle or back of the cushions.
● Pretend to reach and stretch to rescue the ball. Invite your child to join in, encouraging him to actually retrieve the ball.
● Repeat a few times, encouraging your child to choose a 'ball' and roll it, then to reach and bring it back, placing it in the tub.
● If he is ready to try walking, hold his hands and walk with him to the ball or object. Let him bend to pick it up, then go back and sit with him, ready to roll the next item.

Taking it further
● Let your child collect the balls and objects one by one and walk, crawl or shuffle with them to drop them into a large box!
● Encourage your child to exclaim with you each time they drop an object into the box. Describe the different sounds they make as they are dropped. Repeat the game as often as the child wishes!

LEARNING OPPORTUNITIES
● To develop listening skills
● To develop co-ordination
● To develop a sense of movement.

YOU WILL NEED
Five or six cushions or pillows; a selection of toys that make sounds (such as a rattle, drum, bells, squeaky book or animal).

Walk about

Sharing the game
● Place the pillows separately around the floor. On top of each cushion place a toy that makes a noise.
● Hold your child by the hand (or both hands depending on how confident at walking she is).
● Walk with her to the first cushion. Squat down beside it and look at the toy. Encourage her to copy you.
● Let her pick up the toy and encourage her to explore it. If she needs help, show her how to manipulate the toy so that it makes a noise.
● Continue the sound journey, moving to the next cushion and toy. Give your child a small basket to collect the sound makers as they discover each one.
● At the end of her 'journey' let her explore the toys once more. Remind her, if necessary, of how to manipulate them. Join in with her as she exclaims at the sound each one makes.

Taking it further
● Repeat this game outside with different toys.
● Hide the toys under the cushions and encourage your child to stop and find the hidden 'treasure'.
● Make the cushions into high towers, piling a few up with the toys on top. Knock them down together!

AGE RANGE
1-2 years

LEARNING OPPORTUNITIES
● To encourage listening and responding to sounds
● To develop confidence in movement
● To develop a range of physical movements.

YOU WILL NEED
A cassette recorder; a children's musical cassette; a small bright box or basket; a selection of small instruments such as a shaker, maracus, bells, and a tambourine.

Dance to the beat

Sharing the game
● Sit with your baby and listen to some of the music.
● Make movements to illustrate your enjoyment such as tapping your hands on your knees or gently clapping your hands.
● Turn the sound down so that the music is quiet in the background.
● Sit beside the basket of instruments with your child. Allow

him to explore the sounds that the instruments make.
● Choose an instrument, stand up, and invite him to do the same.
● As you tap the instrument gently against your hand or hip, walk to the beat.
● Turn off the background music and gently walk around the space using the instrument to play a familiar tune such as 'Twinkle, Twinkle Little Star' or 'Baa, Baa Black Sheep'. Encourage your child to join in at their own appropriate level, which may be simply to smile, or perhaps to copy your movements.
● Change the instrument and invite your child to swap his.
● Play the music again and dance to the beat! Introduce some wiggles, skips and twirls for your child to try and copy.

Taking it further
● Play a tape of different types of music and walk in different ways to suit the variety of tunes.
● Put on the radio and move to the beat of various types of music.

LEARNING OPPORTUNITIES
● To develop balance and co-ordination
● To encourage making choices
● To enjoy some food tasting.

YOU WILL NEED
Fruit-shaped place mats or coloured card cut into fruit shapes; scissors; small bowls; grapes; strawberries; raisins; apricots.

THINK FIRST!
Make sure that you are aware of any food allergies that your child has. Never leave your child unattended when tasting and eating.

Stepping stones

Sharing the game

● Place your fruit-shaped place mats on the floor to create a path through one room and out into another. Make sure that the mats are placed on surfaces that aren't slippery, such as carpeted areas.
● On every second 'stepping stone', place a bowl with a selection of the fruit pieces.
● Offer a small bowl to your toddler. Take one yourself and begin along the path.
● When you reach a 'stepping stone' that has a bowl, squat beside it and select one piece of fruit from the bowl. Name it and place it in your own bowl. Suggest that your child does the same. Encourage her to select just one piece.
● Repeat the process as you move along the path. Talk about your child's choices with her. Encourage her to wait until the activity is over before she eats her chosen fruits!
● When the selection has been made, sit down together at the end of the path and enjoy your well-deserved snack.

Taking it further

● Suggest that your toddler washes her hands and helps you to place the fruit pieces in the bowls along the stepping stones. Encourage her to talk about what she is doing.
● Play a similar game in the garden. Make a stepping stone path with pieces of material and place pieces of fruit in bowls along the trail. Go together along the path with a basket to gather the fruit!

LEARNING OPPORTUNITIES
● To develop gross motor skills
● To develop the skills of pushing and rolling
● To stimulate the sense of sight.

YOU WILL NEED
Four to five empty plastic bottles; glitter; bright ribbons; food colouring; water; washing-up liquid; sequins.

Push and roll

Sharing the game
● Remove any labels or glue residue from the bottles, by soaking them and then rubbing off the remains.
● Put water in one of your bottles and colour it with food colouring.
● Tie some bright ribbons together and tape them to the underside of the lid of the next bottle, securing the lid.
● In the third bottle, pour less water than in the first and add some large sequins and glitter.
● In the fourth bottle, add water and washing-up liquid. Shake to create bubbles.
● Now let your child explore some movements with the bottles. Encourage him to look at the movements within the bottles first.
● Next, sit opposite your child and roll each bottle to him. Encourage him to roll it back.
● Now try spinning the bottles around in front of your child. Roll each bottle around in front of him. Roll the bottles backwards and forwards without letting go, as though you are using a rolling pin.
● Encourage your child to copy your movements and also to think of his own ways for exploring the bottles.

Taking it further
● Challenge your child to lift and stand each bottle upright.
● Suggest that he places the bottles into a large box or wine carrier.

LET'S GET BUSY

AGE RANGE
2-3 years

LEARNING OPPORTUNITIES
● To develop a sense of beauty
● To use the sense of smell
● To develop hand-to-eye co-ordination.

YOU WILL NEED
Cut flowers of different types, sizes, shapes and colours; small baskets; a large sitting mat; rug.

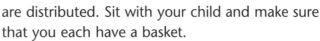

Flower drop

Sharing the game
● Place a variety of different scented and coloured flowers around on a clear floor space, inside or outside.
● Place them at different levels – for example, hanging from a fence or a bush, under a shrub, on a small table, or on the arm of a chair.
● Place a large sitting mat in a clear area, as close as possible to where the flowers are distributed. Sit with your child and make sure that you each have a basket.
● While you are sitting together on the mat, draw your child's attention to the various flowers, commenting on where they are.
● Invite your child to go and collect one and encourage her to bring it back to you.
● Together, gather all the flowers in your baskets. Bring them back to the sitting mat and empty them out. Explore and enjoy the scent of the flowers together.

Taking it further
● Offer your child a jug of water and a vase. Support her while she pours the water in. Then take turns to place the gathered flowers in the vase.
● Look through a magazine together and find some flower pictures. Sniff the pages to find no scent!

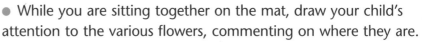

AGE RANGE
2-3 years

LEARNING OPPORTUNITIES
● To develop co-ordination
● To encourage gross motor skills and movement
● To enjoy tasting fruit and cereal.

YOU WILL NEED
A range of small empty boxes; pieces of fruit; small pieces of chocolate; cheese snacks; cereal pieces; pieces of brightly-coloured string; a tapestry needle (for adult use); bowls.

Pull along

Sharing the game
● Remove any lids or top sections from your small boxes, so that you can see down into each box (which will become train carriages).
● Thread some string through your tapestry needle and tie a knot in one end. Sew the boxes together in a line, by piercing holes through the sides of each box and sewing through the middle of them. Tie off the string when you have pierced through the last box to create your chain of 'carriages'.

● Encourage your child to wash his hands at the same time as you.
● Place the pieces of fruit in one bowl, the pieces of chocolate in another and the cheese snacks and cereal pieces in a third. Let your child watch or help.
● Sit with your child and invite him to place some of the snacks into the 'train' to be transported to the area where you will eat them.
● Help him line the train up, and suggest he pulls it to the 'snack' area.
● Support him in manoeuvring the train around any obstacles.
● Encourage him to lift the 'carriages' onto a table, helping when necessary.
● Enjoy the snack together.

Taking it further
● Use the train to encourage you child to tidy up his toys. Alternatively, suggest that he fills the carriages with some books to share together.
● Place his toothbrush, toothpaste, and flannel in the carriages and let him take it into the bathroom at bath time.

AGE RANGE
2-3 years

LEARNING OPPORTUNITIES
● To encourage appreciation of different materials
● To explore and experiment with a variety of surfaces
● To develop a sense of sound.

YOU WILL NEED
A wooden car; a plastic car; a metal car (vary the sizes of the cars); a box; a length of carpet; a length of plastic sheeting; a length of sandpaper; a bamboo place mat or table runner; a cushion.

Car run

Sharing the game
● Tell your child that you are going to make some really exciting roadways to put some toy cars on. Tell her that they will all feel different and sound different when the cars go across them. Show her your set of materials and let her explore them.
● Now invite your child to help you set up the game.
● Place the box, with the various cars inside it, onto the floor.
● Place the length of carpet and the length of sandpaper next to each other, near to the box of cars.
● Choose a car yourself and encourage your child to choose one too. Show her how to move the cars on the different surfaces, talking about what you are doing, as you play. Explain that the carpet and sandpaper are your roadways.
● Now experiment with the other materials. Place the bamboo runner across the sandpaper material to create a crossroads. Then try placing a cushion under one of the 'roads' to create a hill or bumpy road.
● Talk to your child about the variety of sounds created as the cars travel along the different surfaces.

Taking it further
● Use a wooden and metal spoon to tap or run along the roadways. What sounds do they make? Do the spoons make the same sounds as the cars?
● Run a scarf or piece of soft fabric along each of the roadways to test whether you can hear any sound being made.

LEARNING OPPORTUNITIES
● To encourage stretching and reaching
● To develop ability to build and balance objects of different sizes
● To develop awareness of texture.

YOU WILL NEED
Sofa cushions; pillows; small scented pillows; hand towels; face cloths; and pillowcases.

Pile up

Sharing the game
● Suggest that your child helps you to create a soft area to play in. Ask him to think of all the soft objects from around the house that he might use.
● Go on a hunt together to find soft cushions, pillows and pillowcases, towels and so on. Talk about the softness and different textures of each thing.
● Choose a suitable place and put all the gathered soft objects on the floor.
● Show your child how to pile one or two of the objects on top of each other.
● Suggest that he helps you to add a few more.
● Now explain that you are going to make a large tower together, using the large pillows and then the cushions. Show him how you need to put the largest things on the bottom first. Next, place the smaller cushions to create a large 'tower'.
● Talk about the different textures, colours and weights of the objects in the 'tower'.

● Now show your child what happens when you start with the smallest object! Balance a small cushion on its side and challenge your child to place a larger one on top. Let it topple over as he piles the cushions on top.
● Finally, challenge your child to return all the pillows, cushions and other soft things back to their original places.

Taking it further
● Hide a few of his toys between some of the pillows.
● Make a small pile of cushions, and then invite your child to help you build a tower from bricks. Challenge him to make the tower taller than the cushion pile.

TOUCH

Of all the sensory experiences, touch is the foremost means of letting your newborn baby know he is loved. It is essential to development. As well as touch being a sense of comfort, it offers a sense of security and reassurance in new situations and environments. Holding, caressing and massaging is an intimate way to build a strong and lasting relationship with your baby.

YOUR NEW BABY

When your baby enters the world you will be in close physical contact with him. Most new parents automatically touch, caress and cuddle their new baby. This intimacy encourages bonding. The sense of touch being stimulated between you and your child is a lovely and most natural way to spend your first hours together.

How you can help

● While your baby is awake, interact with him. Chat to him, look at him and be near him. If you are packing the washing machine, let him watch and tell him what you are doing. If you are watching a television programme then involve him by sitting close and looking at him and tickling him.

● Remember that to be close and build a relationship with your baby does not mean you have to pick him up and hold him all the time. It means you have to relate to him, involve him and engage him.

USING HIS MOUTH TO EXPLORE

When your baby uses his sense of touch, the sense nerves send signals to his brain stimulating its growth. By using his mouth to explore objects your baby's brain will be developing new connections and interconnections. Your baby is not looking to eat the objects he is placing in his mouth, rather, he is trying to explore them. Remember that it is fine for him to explore appropriate objects using his mouth, but always be on hand to ensure that unsuitable items are not explored in this way. Be gentle when encouraging your baby to give up an unsuitable object – try not to make the removal a negative experience.

How you can help

● Keep his environment safe and free from any items that will cause him harm.

● Offer him objects and toys that can be explored using his mouth. If it shouldn't actually be put in his mouth, then show distaste by your expression and gentle but firm tone of voice.

● Give him access to a range of tasting opportunities to stimulate his sense of touch. He will find it pleasant to use his mouth to explore items such as a spoon with milk on (or other foodstuff, allergy and age-dependent) or a bowl of small pieces of bread.

ROUTINES

Every time you change a nappy or put your baby down to sleep you promote bonding. You do this by placing him in a physical area that is warm, soft, and cosy. The softness of a wipe, the coolness of a cream, the warmth of a clean nappy, are all experienced through his sense of touch. Having experienced this routine he has had his needs met and he feels secure that he is cared for. As his internal model of the world evolves he can also predict what may happen next and be comfortable in his predictions.

How you can help
● Every family approaches these routines in a different way – there is no perfect answer. Getting to know your child and what he needs and enjoys will help you to create the routine that is best for you both. Remember to take the opportunity to build a close relationship by including touch and closeness as a part of these routines.

THE ENVIRONMENT

Encourage your baby to experience a variety of textures visually and through touch (by picking up, feeling and shaking the object for example).

How you can help
● Gather some collections of textured items, such as a set of natural items – fir cones, a wooden spoon, driftwood and pebbles. Let your child explore them.
● Introduce new fabrics on a regular basis. They could be scarves, a cushion cover or a towel, for example.
● Add items such as sand, bubbles or pebbles into a small bowl of water for him to explore.
● Go outside and touch the flowers, grass, bushes, tree bark.

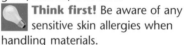 **Think first!** Be aware of any sensitive skin allergies when handling materials.

MANIPULATION SKILLS

In the first three years of life your baby will have gained a great deal of information and knowledge from 'touching' his world.

From three months old he may be reaching and grasping for objects. Introduce a wide variety of textures for him to play with. He will soon pick items up, lifting them to suck, using his tongue and lips to touch and gain information from. By nine months he will not just pick up but have the ability to let go and drop items. If you place textures below

and around him he will happily try out his newly acquired skills! As well as the touch sensations that he will experience he will also hear the sounds that the objects make when held, manipulated and dropped. As your baby learns to eat finger foods and feed himself he will be exposed to a new range of manipulating opportunities that he will get thoroughly immersed in (quite literally, at times!). He will be keen to build with bricks – introduce cardboard, wooden and plastic bricks to allow him to explore a range of textures.

When moving into his second year your child will continue to use hands-on adventures to gain insights into his world. During his adventures there will be spaces and equipment he should not touch. This will take time to establish and until he is into his third or even fourth year, he will have trouble remembering limits and boundaries. Be patient with him, explaining why you have said 'no'. Repeat this often and eventually he will respond to the boundaries you have set.

This will allow him in his third and fourth years to use his well-developed sense of touch to make more sense of his environment. He will continue to manipulate the objects he comes into contact with during each of the play situations he is involved in, learning as he does so.

How you can help
● Offer a wide range of everyday items for your child to play with, not just toys.
● Present opportunities for him to manipulate objects in different ways such as dropping, posting, squashing and squeezing.
● Set challenges such as doing up buttons, twirling spaghetti round a spoon and hanging hoops round a post.

TOUCH

LEARNING OPPORTUNITIES
● To visually stimulate
● To introduce a variety of textures
● To encourage exploration.

YOU WILL NEED
Fabric in a variety of different lengths and textures; a few boxes covered in colourful fabric; a basket; a few favourite toys.

In my space

Sharing the game
● Create an interesting space for your baby to explore. Drape some fabric over some boxes or furniture and place a few colourful boxes on the floor. Add a basket with some favourite toys in it and place a few large toys in 'hiding places' behind the sofa, under a chair, behind the curtains and so on.

● Make a tent by draping fabric lengths between tables and chairs or the sofa and a bookcase, for example. Ensure that the furniture cannot be pulled over by the weight of the draped fabric. Vary the textures and colours of the fabric – perhaps a piece of animal print fabric, some suede and some cotton.

● Now invite your child to come with you and explore the space, either by crawling, toddling or simply in your arms. Show him how to touch, squeeze, feel and stroke the different fabrics. Talk about the colours and textures as you explore the environment.

● Show your baby the tent and go inside it together. Let the fabric brush against you and encourage your baby to feel the fabrics against his face and body as well as in his hands. Name the colours of the fabrics and describe any patterns.

● Now let your baby explore freely and watch him as he does so. Does he copy any of the ideas you suggested?

Taking it further
● Make up a mini-environment for your child to explore. Take a large box and place flower fabric inside. Add some silk flowers, a flower cushion, and a soft toy flower inside. Let your baby spend time exploring all the items.

● In a blue box, place some blue fabric and some blue items such as a brush, flannel, sock, teddy and ribbon.

TOUCH

LEARNING OPPORTUNITIES
● To encourage exploration of textures
● To stimulate natural curiosity
● To develop vocabulary.

YOU WILL NEED
Five or six shoe boxes; samples of fabric and other materials such as sandpaper, corrugated card, towelling, fake fur, cord, bubble wrap, felt pieces.

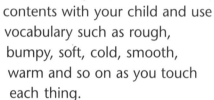

In the box

Sharing the game

● Remove the lids from the shoe boxes and line them up in a row on a low table or the floor (whichever your baby will find easiest and safest to access).

● Make a felt 'lid' for each box by cutting a piece of felt slightly bigger than the box and taping it to the box at one end so that it can be lifted like a flap.

● Place a sample of fabric or material in the bottom of each box and cover them all over with their felt lids.

● Sit with your baby and encourage her to place her hand under the flap of each box in turn, exploring the contents by touch. Feel the contents with your child and use vocabulary such as rough, bumpy, soft, cold, smooth, warm and so on as you touch each thing.

● Although your baby will not have the vocabulary to respond to some of your more complicated questions it is still worth asking her as she can understand a lot more than she can say at this stage. She will be soaking up all you can tell her! Ask questions such as, 'Which one do you like?'; 'Can you find the rough one?' and so on. You may be surprised by her responses!

Taking it further

● Place objects of opposite texture onto the floor such as a rough nail brush and a soft face cloth; a smooth bath toy and a rough bath scrunchy. Let your baby explore them.

● Place items of different textures into the shoe boxes so that your baby can explore various textures at the same time.

TOUCH

LEARNING OPPORTUNITIES
● To explore different textures
● To develop balance and co-ordination.

YOU WILL NEED
A selection of rough and smooth fabrics or materials, such as pieces of felt, a plastic carrier bag, bubble wrap, fake fur fabric, suede or leather, sandpaper, linoleum and a carpet tile.

Texture this

Sharing the game
● Gather the range of materials and cut each piece into tile shapes (25 x 25cm is ideal).
● Vary the textures so that the line contrasts between soft, rough, smooth, crinkly and so on. For example you might place fake fur, followed by sandpaper, then linoleum followed by carpet.
● Use your path of tiles for some exploration with hands and feet.
● Take care with materials such as sandpaper that your baby does not graze or cut his hands or knees. Move him around rough materials if necessary.
● Take your baby's hand and go for a walk, carry or crawl along the path. Encourage him to bend down and touch each of the textures with his hands.
● Now take your baby's socks and shoes off and walk along again. Encourage him to feel the textures on his bare feet.
● Spend some time exploring each texture. Are some tickly? Are some soft and cuddly? As your baby touches each one describe it by texture, colour and so on.

Taking it further
● Use the path as a track for cars. Which materials make it easy to push the cars? Which ones are a bit difficult? Your baby will have to work out that he needs to push the cars harder on certain materials and that other materials, such as the linoleum, are good surfaces for whizzing cars on!

TOUCH

LEARNING OPPORTUNITIES
● To encourage exploration of hard and soft textures
● To introduce new vocabulary
● To develop fine motor skills.

YOU WILL NEED
A large saucepan; a hob or cooker; a plastic mat; a range of types of dried pasta including spaghetti; two bowls; food colouring.

THINK FIRST!
Never leave a baby unattended when eating and handling food.

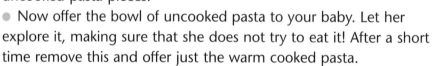

Tasty time

Sharing the game
● Place a plastic mat on the floor for your baby to sit on. Let your baby watch while you select a variety of pasta shapes. Tell her that you will be putting them into a saucepan to cook them.
● Cook the pasta according to the instructions, drain and leave it to cool down a little.
● Place the warm pasta in a large bowl. In another bowl place a selection of uncooked pasta pieces.
● Now offer the bowl of uncooked pasta to your baby. Let her explore it, making sure that she does not try to eat it! After a short time remove this and offer just the warm cooked pasta.
● When your baby has explored both bowls individually return the other bowl and let her explore them simultaneously, enabling direct comparisons.
● Explore the two bowls together and talk about the different textures. Describe how each type of pasta feels, smells and looks.
● Talk about how it is difficult to handle some of the pieces of cooked pasta. Encourage development of your baby's fine motor skills by asking her to handle small and slippery pieces!

Taking it further
● Use different coloured pasta shapes and add some grated cheese to the cooked pasta.
● Use jelly or milky pudding instead of pasta.

AGE RANGE
1-2 years

LEARNING OPPORTUNITIES
● To explore contrasting textures
● To mix liquid and powder
● To develop control of small muscles.

YOU WILL NEED
Two large bowls; flour; water; cornflour; water spray container; plastic table cover; two large trays; a cup.

Mix and squash

Sharing the game

● Pour some cornflour onto one of the large trays. Take it to your child who is sitting on the plastic table cover on the floor.
● Encourage your child to touch the dry powder. Add some water and ask your child to feel it now.
● Take one of the bowls yourself and give the other to your child.
● Sit with your child on the plastic cover. Place some flour into each bowl, describing it as you do so.
● Explore the soft, cool powder.
● Dribble some flour into your palm and then his.
● Hold on to the flour in one hand and spray water into your other hand. Ask your child to do the same, spraying the water for them if necessary. Your child will probably find the water spray quite irresistible! Let him have a turn at spraying the water (in a controlled way), and ask him to spray the flour in your hand or bowl.

● Now show your child how to squash your watery and floury hands together to create a sticky handful.
● Next, place the two trays on the plastic mat on the floor. Pour a cup full of cornflour onto each tray. Use the water spray to dampen the cornflour.
● Enjoy the 'sticky mixture'!

Taking it further

● Add some food colour to the mixture. Encourage your child to mix the colour in and call his attention to the changing colour and texture.
● Offer your child a pot of glitter to sprinkle into the mixture. Watch and encourage your child as he mixes and manipulates the mixture.

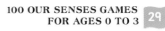

TOUCH

LEARNING OPPORTUNITIES
● To develop understanding of the concept of wet and dry
● To touch and explore cold solids and liquids
● To introduce vocabulary to describe textures.

YOU WILL NEED
Ice cube trays; water; a freezer; glitter; a few flowers; a leaf; a small plastic animal; three or four small bowls; a large bowl; a tablespoon.

THINK FIRST!
● Ice cubes present a serious choking hazard to babies and young children. Make sure that your child does not place the ice cubes in her mouth.

Ice play

Sharing the game
● Fill the ice cube trays with water. In a few of the compartments add some extra things. For example, add glitter, a flower petal, a leaf and a plastic animal to some of the compartments.
● Put the ice trays in the freezer and wait for the cubes to be ready.
● When the cubes are frozen, pop them out into the small bowls for your child to explore.
● Warn your child not to hold the cubes for too long, as ice can hurt and stick to the skin.

● Encourage her to describe what she can see in the different ice cubes. Let her touch the cubes briefly and provide her with some words to describe what she can feel – wet, slippery, hard and so on.
● Fill the large bowl with warm water. Suggest that your child carefully adds the cubes to the warm water. Provide her with a spoon and help her to transfer the cubes, one by one.
● Watch or come back later to see that the ice cubes have melted. Look at the plastic animal, petal, leaf and so on that remain in the water.

Taking it further
● Make ice cubes from diluted fruit juice. Place them in a bowl for your child to see. Use straws to drink the icy juice when melted.
● Add some petals and leaves to a bowl of water and freeze it. Watch the ice melt leaving the petals and leaves to float in the water.

AGE RANGE
1-2 years

LEARNING OPPORTUNITIES
● To stimulate the sense of smell
● To explore and become familiar with a variety of natural textures
● To create a texture 'picture'.

YOU WILL NEED
Fresh flowers; herbs; petals; grasses; twigs; pot pourri; citrus fruit peel; large pieces of paper or card; paper plates; glue or sticky backed paper.

THINK FIRST!
Make sure that your child is not sensitive to any of the materials. Allergies such as eczema may be irritated by grasses, for example.

Nature collage

Sharing the game
● Take each of the natural items and place them on pieces of paper or paper plates on the floor.
● Lift each of the items separately. Name each one, smell it and offer it to your toddler. Suggest that he explores the item by touching and smelling it. Describe the item to your child as he explores it.
● Repeat the process with each of the items.
● Roll out a large sheet of sticky backed paper or spread some glue onto a sheet of ordinary paper.
● Suggest that your child chooses some of the items to place on the sticky surface of the paper to create a textured, scented piece of art.

Taking it further
● Go into the garden and gather some natural items in a bucket or basket. Sit on the grass and explore the things. Place them out to create a tree or flower or face.
● Choose some flowers to press. Use a flower press or simply place the flowers between some sheets of plain or blotting paper and put inside a heavy book,. Place some other books on top and leave the flowers for a few days. Take the book out and open the page. Let your child lift the pressed flowers and test whether they still have a scent.

TOUCH

LEARNING OPPORTUNITIES
● To explore the textures of containers
● To encourage curiosity
● To develop hand-to-eye co-ordination.

YOU WILL NEED
Five or six empty tissue boxes with different patterns on the outside or a range of different fabrics to cover the boxes; scissors; glue. A range of items to place inside the various boxes as described in the activity.

Tissue box

Sharing the game
● Use empty tissue boxes with different patterns. Alternatively cover the boxes with fur, linen, tartan fabric, towelling and so on.
● Place a variety of objects inside each box, choosing items that reflect the decorative outside of the boxes. For example, inside a box covered in holographic paper, place lengths of shiny ribbon, some large shiny buttons, and empty shiny sweet wrappers. Or, inside a box covered in tartan fabric, place swatches of tartan fabric, tartan ribbon and some heather.
● Encourage your toddler to explore the contents of each box. Explore the boxes with your child, showing her how to wrap ribbons around her fingers, rub fabric on her cheek, smell the flowers, roll the pebbles and so on. Your child may start to copy what you do. Remember to praise her for all her efforts!

Taking it further
● Empty the contents from each box and then begin to refill the boxes. Suggest that your child helps you to put everything back again. Repeat this game with a few of the boxes you have created.
● Rummage with your child in a few drawers and cupboards to find new things to add to your collections. Hide some safe things ready for her to find.

TOUCH

LEARNING OPPORTUNITIES
● To introduce the concept of rough and smooth
● To encourage sorting items
● To explore textured items.

YOU WILL NEED
One large empty cardboard box; a variety of fabric; two trays or two small baskets; a variety of rough and smooth items (see activity for suggestions).

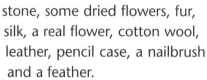

Rough and smooth

Sharing the game
● Place a large piece of rough fabric such as hessian on the bottom of the large box.
● Cover the rest of the box with different fabric textures.
● Now choose a variety of rough and smooth items to place inside the box. Ideas include bark, a fir cone, pumice stone, a precious stone, some dried flowers, fur, silk, a real flower, cotton wool, leather, pencil case, a nailbrush and a feather.

● Invite your child to touch all the sides of the box. Talk about the different textures of the fabric together.
● Now invite your child to touch and explore the objects inside the box. As you and your child explore each item, name them and describe them, using the words rough and smooth.
● Offer your child the two trays or baskets and suggest that he places all the rough objects in one basket and all the smooth objects in the other one.
● Help and support your child with the sorting when invited.

Taking it further
● Take him into the bathroom to find one smooth item and one rough. Then take him into the garden and find one of each there. Add them to the collection you already have.
● Place two smooth objects onto a small tray. Make a point of saying, 'A smooth stone, a smooth piece of cloth'. Ask him to choose another smooth object to add to your collection. Do not correct him if he gets it wrong. Repeat the activity at a later date and note if your child has made the distinction.

AGE RANGE ●●●
2-3 years

LEARNING
OPPORTUNITIES
● To explore dough and manipulate by kneading and stretching
● To encourage experimentation.

YOU WILL NEED
A large amount of basic dough (see recipe on page 125); four small bowls; four small plates; sugar; glitter; peppermint essence; baby oil.

Dough not!

Sharing the game

● Make a basic dough mix and place it in a large bowl.
● Explore the dough with the child, encourage her to pinch it, stretch it, roll it, and break it.
● Suggest that you make four little piles, ask her to help you. Split the mix with her help and place it on four small plates.
● Take the four small bowls and place sugar in one, glitter in another, peppermint essence in the next and baby oil in the last.

● Encourage her to dip a lump of dough into each bowl. Experiment and play with the four different textures which have now been created.

Taking it further

● Encourage her to use the dough to make simple shapes such as a sausage and a coin. Show her how to manipulate the dough to make round, flat and sausage shapes. Let her create a shape and ask her about it, saying 'Tell me all about your shape, it's great!'.
● Challenge her to guess which one of the doughs you have. Hide it in your closed hand and let her sniff or touch it. Then let her see it and find out if she was right.

TOUCH

LEARNING OPPORTUNITIES
● To use a variety of materials creatively to explore colour
● To develop an awareness of soft materials becoming hard.

YOU WILL NEED
Pudding paint (see recipe on page 126); paper plates; powder paint (in a variety of colours); junk materials; glitter; wooden spoons; sequins; feathers; twigs and so on.

Paint pots

Sharing the game
● Make some pudding paint, following the recipe on page 126.
● Invite your child to help you stir it round in a large bowl. Talk together about the way it feels, looks and smells.
● Place the powder paints and glitter onto the paper plates.
● Invite him to choose some paint. Each time he adds some, help him to stir it into the mixture.
● Allow him to experiment with the glitter.
● Once the pudding paint is ready, suggest that your child uses his fingers to apply some of the mixture onto one of the larger pieces of junk, such as an eggbox or cardboard tube.
● Once he has 'painted' the piece of junk, you can help him to select and add some of the other materials, such as the sequins, feathers and so on.
● Let the model dry overnight. Exclaim over the masterpiece together in the morning!

Taking it further
● Use Mod Roc (purchase in art stores and follow the instructions) or papier mâché to create an interesting model.
● Make a sculpture from lots of small junk pieces by taping or sticking them together using glue or sticky tape.

TOUCH

LEARNING OPPORTUNITIES
● To investigate a range of colours
● To develop problem solving skills
● To develop matching skills.

YOU WILL NEED
Strong card in three colours (such as red, blue, green); scissors; lots of small fabric scraps in your three chosen colours; glue; a small basket.

Jigsaw pieces

Sharing the game
● Cut out two large circles from each piece of coloured card.
● Take one circle of each of the colours and cut each one into three pieces. The pieces do not need to be equal and each colour does not need to be cut into the same shapes.
● Take the first colour (say, red) and choose three different shades of red fabric. Glue the fabric to the three puzzle pieces you have already cut out, to make a textured puzzle.
● Repeat this with the other two colours. You will now have three complete card circles and three sets of puzzle pieces.
● Place the nine jigsaw pieces into the basket.
● Invite your child to choose one of the whole circles. Now ask her to find the three matching coloured pieces from the basket. Challenge her to use the pieces to cover the circle without any gaps.
● Join in the game, choosing a different colour.
● Finally, suggest that your child attempts to complete all three puzzles by herself (offering help, of course, if required).

Taking it further
● Create another set of jigsaws in a different shape, such as a square. Use some other textures such as sandpaper, corrugated card and so on for these.

One of your baby's basic needs is, of course, food. One of his first natural reflexes is sucking (and therefore feeding). From his first days, your baby will reach out and touch you – he will watch you, smell you and listen to you. Taste is a sense that is often left to develop only at feeding time. You can aid this development by providing play activities involving taste.

TASTE

FOOD AND DRINK

Naturally, the primary taste sensations come from the consumption of food and drink. Statistics would lead us to believe that we are a nation of unhealthy eaters. For many people today, convenient fast foods, microwave meals and 'TV dinners' have taken over the ritual of sitting down as a family for home-cooked meals. This need not be the case for you and your child, and mealtimes can become a happy and bonding experience with just a little bit of time and energy. The suggestions in this chapter may help you to achieve this.

HEALTHY EATING

Right from the beginning it is of great value to teach your child the benefits of healthy eating. Our attitudes to food will naturally influence our children's and we should offer very positive experiences of food and eating. By introducing a wide variety of different foods through positive play opportunities, even the youngest child will begin to form good eating habits, which will have a positive impact on his future health.

Learning about food should be fun. There are no rules for introducing the five food groups and there is no reason to find snack and meal times as something to dread. Like all areas of development each child will do things at different rates. Remember

How you can help

● Sit together and eat. Make snack and meal times an important part of your child's day. Remember it shouldn't matter how long it takes, try not to rush, but enjoy!
● Talk through what is happening as you prepare the food. Talk about the tastes he is about to experience using positive 'tasty' words such as 'juicy', 'creamy' and 'sweet'.
● Let your child help with washing fruit and vegetables before you prepare them. Let him gather the cutlery and set the table.
● Suggest that he selects the plates and utensils you will need and encourage him to watch as you serve the food.

your child is an individual and his likes and dislikes will not necessarily be the same as yours or his siblings.

How you can help

● Carry out tasting activities at snack times. Place four or five fruit pieces on a plate and encourage him to taste each one. Do the same with different types of breads, cereals and drinks.

● Let him try different foods from all five food groups, ensuring that he has a balance throughout the day.

● Even with baby food, try to introduce new tastes into his diet. But remember to let him get used to and develop a taste for the foods you give him.

● A range of different tasting and textured puddings should be offered.

● Try to avoid fatty and sweet foods. However, in moderation these foods will do him no harm.

PLAYING WITH FOOD

Like everything new, your baby will want to explore and experiment with his food. This is a vital part of his getting to know and enjoy all foods. Try not to be over anxious when he pours or smudges his food around or refuses to taste something. It is important that you relax. Offer a range of items and if he refuses something, offer him an alternative from the same food group. On another occasion offer the refused item for him to try again. This will encourage a variety in his diet and will lead to a relaxed attitude towards food both new or familiar.

How you can help

● Food is not just about taste. Young children need to explore using their sense of touch and smell. Let them experience food in this way.

● Place a large quantity of cooked pasta in a bowl for him to play with. Let him use his hands, spoons, forks and so on.

● Put some jelly or milky pudding on a low table or tray for him to explore. Be aware that not all young children will enjoy the sensation of food in this way. Never force your child, but encourage him to explore by leading the way. Roll up your sleeves and tuck in!

● Carry out play activities that involve food or drink. They can link into your normal routine so that your child will approach them in a relaxed frame of mind. This way they may be more willing to try out something new.

ROUTINES

Just as a routine for sleeping, changing and bathing is important, it is the same with meal times or snack times. Remember that young children need regular meals and may need small healthy snacks in between. If you offer as wide a variety as possible, it is more than likely that you will be providing a 'balanced diet'. It is essential, of course, that you offer foods containing protein and carbohydrates to ensure your child's growth and development.

The eating of food is not the only opportunity here. Involving your child in the preparation of snacks is also valuable. Under your close supervision your child will also learn a lot about personal and food hygiene. They will benefit from watching and listening to you and will feel proud about helping you.

Involving your child in the various activities suggested in this chapter will provide the chance for him to develop a broad range of skills, from fine and gross motor skill development to the absorption of new vocabulary. He will have the opportunity to explore texture, experiment with taste and make choices. Some of the suggested activities will encourage your child to share, take turns, investigate new food and try new flavours. But most of all by taking part in these activities your child will get the chance to develop, in his own time, a healthy and positive regard for food.

How you can help

● Wash hands together and let your child wash the apple, pear, grapes or other fruit that you are having as a snack.

● Have regular times for snacks, such as after their favourite morning television programme, or when older siblings come home from school, and emphasise the time for meals, 'It's half past twelve – time for lunch'.

● Encourage them to choose what to have in a sandwich and help to make it.

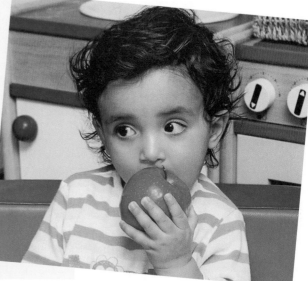

TASTE

LEARNING OPPORTUNITIES
● To explore the texture of food
● To experiment with spoons
● To taste a variety of cold puddings.

YOU WILL NEED
A plastic floor cover sheet; baby's high chair; paper plates; spoons; pink custard; chocolate yoghurt and yellow dessert (ready mixed).

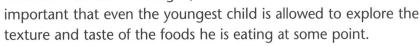

Custard and yoghurt

Sharing the game
● Sit with your baby on the plastic sheet, alternatively sit your baby in his high chair and pull up a chair alongside him. Make sure that you have both washed your hands.
● Pour the custard, yoghurt and so on onto separate paper plates or directly onto the high chair tray.
● Allow baby to explore each plate separately. If he seems hesitant, demonstrate by dipping one finger tip in. Smell and taste.

● Offer a spoon for the baby to spread out the various puddings. Take one yourself and again demonstrate.
● Add a spoonful of yoghurt to the custard and allow him to experiment too.
● If he chooses to use his fingers and hands then allow him to explore in this way, creating a 'tasty mess'.
● While playing with food at mealtimes is not encouraged, it is important that even the youngest child is allowed to explore the texture and taste of the foods he is eating at some point.
● Call attention to the texture, colour and taste of each of the puddings he chooses to explore.

Taking it further
● Place the food in bowls and invite your baby to try and spoon them from the bowl onto the plate or tray, ready to explore.
● At the end of the activity give him a cloth to help you clean up. Explain what you are doing while you clean together.

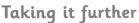

TASTE

LEARNING OPPORTUNITIES
● To introduce a range of flavours
● To explore cold, textured food
● To develop hand-to-eye co-ordination.

YOU WILL NEED
Three bowls; vanilla ice-cream; raspberry ripple ice-cream and ice-cream with a rough texture such as raisins or oatmeal; six spoons.

Ice-cream dream

Sharing the game
● Choose the different ice-cream flavours and place a small amount of each one in the three bowls.
● If possible, before showing them to your baby, cover them with another set of bowls or something appropriate.
● Place them on a low table or floor mat.
● Choose one bowl and slowly uncover it in front of your baby. Exclaim with appropriate language at what you have discovered under the 'lid'.

● Wait and watch to see if your baby 'removes' the other lids to find the ice-cream dreams inside!
● Talk about the flavours, as you offer each one to your baby.
● Let her feed herself if she is able.
● If she plays with the food, try not to get stressed!

Taking it further
● Place a selection of flakes of banana, raisins, small pieces of wafer and marshmallow pieces onto a plate. Suggest that your baby adds these to the ice-cream. Taste the different things and comment on the texture of each one.
● Offer a spoon for her to use. Stir, lift or add the small items to the ice-cream.
● Offer your baby the opportunity to add fruit pieces to her yoghurt the next time she is eating one.

TASTE

AGE RANGE
0-1 year

LEARNING OPPORTUNITIES
● To explore by taste a range of foods
● To develop hand-to-eye co-ordination
● To develop an awareness of language.

YOU WILL NEED
Four bowls; green jelly; milky pudding with raisins, apricots and strawberries; blancmange; sponge cake; a low table or picnic mat.

Pudding texture

Sharing the game
● Place a large lump of jelly in one bowl, a large portion of blancmange in another, the sponge cake in a third and the milky pudding in the fourth bowl.
● Sit beside your baby, so that he can watch you prepare the bowls.
● Let him see you place the raisins and cut the other fruits into small pieces, then add them to the milky pudding.

● While you are preparing each bowl describe what you are doing. Stop and say your child's name and ask him if he is watching. What can he see?
● Place each of the bowls on a low table or a picnic mat.
● Take a spoon and gently break up the jelly while he watches. Offer him some. Repeat this with each food.
● Lift the sponge and offer him a 'bite'.
● Now allow him to explore with his spoon and enjoy the tastes. While he explores, describe the textures and tastes he is experiencing.
● Make sure he doesn't eat too much!

Taking it further
● Invite your baby to help you to ice a large sponge cake. Let him help you mix up some icing sugar, water and food colouring to the right consistency. Show him how to help you spread the icing over the cake with the back of a spoon.

TASTE

LEARNING OPPORTUNITIES
● To develop hand-to-eye co-ordination
● To explore a different method of eating (dipping)
● To enjoy a variety of tastes.

YOU WILL NEED
Soft toast; croissant; brown bread; roll; yoghurt; soft cheese; light garlic dip; hummus; plates and bowls.

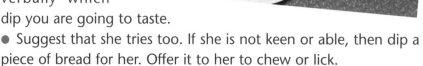

Bread dip

Sharing the game
● Prepare the breads and dips in an area where your baby can watch you, perhaps at the table with baby in the highchair or on the floor.
● Cut the various breads into strips, small enough for your baby to chew on and hold.
● Stir each of the dips with a spoon. Smell each one as you stir it and offer it towards your baby to smell.
● Once you have stirred each of the dips, place the plate with the various bread strips beside the bowls.
● Sit with your baby, choose a strip, naming it and then ponder verbally which dip you are going to taste.
● Suggest that she tries too. If she is not keen or able, then dip a piece of bread for her. Offer it to her to chew or lick.
● If she just wants to play with it, then allow her to explore in her own way.
● Repeat the process with each of the breads and dips.
● Join in – if she sees you experimenting she will gain the confidence to try for herself.

Taking it further
● Use a knife to spread some of the dips along the bread strips. While you are spreading each dip, talk about the smell. Say things such as, 'I can't wait to taste it! This one smells really cheesy and tasty!'.

AGE RANGE
1-2 years

LEARNING OPPORTUNITIES
● To taste a variety of fruits
● To create a simple snack
● To develop hand-to-eye co-ordination.

YOU WILL NEED
Grapes; strawberries; banana; pineapple; cheese spread; cheese; butter; small bowls; plates; brown and white bread.

Fruit bread

Sharing the game

● Involve your child in washing the fruit. Chop the fruit into small pieces. Place them in a range of small bowls.
● Spread a little butter or cheese spread onto small slices of bread.
● Sit with your child and suggest that you make some fruit bread to enjoy together.
● Choose a piece of bread and place it on your plate. Suggest that he does this too.
● Show each of the bowls of fruit to your child, naming each fruit as you go. Let him touch, smell and taste the fruits.
● Tell your child that you are going to put a piece of each fruit on your bread to make a fruity sandwich!
● Help him to create his own choice of fruit bread and then enjoy them together.
● For the next piece, suggest that you are going to place a piece of cheese, followed by a slice of banana with a grape on the top! Can your child copy you?

● Help your child to make an arrangement of his choice and then enjoy your next slice together!

Taking it further

● Toast some of the bread then spread some butter and mashed banana onto it.
● Cut one of the pieces of toast into slices and dip them into some soft cheese or chocolate spread.

LEARNING OPPORTUNITIES
● To introduce the concept of spreading
● To introduce the idea of choosing
● To further develop the sense of taste.

YOU WILL NEED
Bread; toaster; butter; jam; cheese spread; honey; lemon curd; an adult's spreading knife and one for a child; spoons; plates and napkins.

Strips of toast

Sharing the game
● Toast a few slices of bread then cut them into slices.
● Place the selection of spreads on a table, still in their jars and tubs.
● While they remain closed, hand each one to your toddler to look at and explore. Stay close by as they handle any glass jars.
● Talk about the pictures and words on the labels, the lids, what the container is made of and so on.
● Open one of the containers, saying what it is. Spoon a small amount onto a toast strip. Use your adult knife to spread it.
● Now offer the spoon to her to do the same. Help her if necessary and again, exclaim at the smell and taste.
● Repeat the process with the various spreads.
● Remember, although you should try to allow your toddler to do as much of this as possible independently, you should be realistic and help her with anything she cannot do.

Taking it further
● Play a tasting matching game. Give your child a spoon of spread to taste or smell. Can she match it to the jar it came from?

AGE RANGE
1-2 years

LEARNING OPPORTUNITIES
● To use mark making to create a pattern
● To develop small muscle control
● To develop hand-to-eye co-ordination.

YOU WILL NEED
Sponge fingers; digestive biscuits or crackers; icing sugar; paper bags; spoons; jug of water; food colouring; plates and a mixing bowl.

Drizzle biscuits

Sharing the game
● Put the packets of biscuits onto a surface, next to a large plate.
● Encourage your child to select a few from each packet and place them onto the plate.
● Put some icing sugar into the mixing bowl.
● Help your child to pour a small amount of water from the jug into the bowl.
● Support him as he mixes the contents, adding more icing sugar or water as required. Add a drop of colouring.

● Take the mixture and spoon a little into the corners of two paper bags. Snip small holes into the corners of the bags. The icing sugar mixture needs to be slightly runny so that it can drizzle out of the holes easily.
● Give your child one of the icing bags and keep one for yourself.
● Show your child how to drizzle the icing onto the biscuits and sponge fingers. Let him have a turn.
● Repeat the activity with a different colour of icing.

Taking it further
● Cut out a coaster and place-mat from thick card. Drizzle some paint onto the card to make brightly coloured splash patterns. If possible, laminate them or cover them in sticky-backed plastic and use them at mealtimes.

TASTE

AGE RANGE
1-2 years

LEARNING OPPORTUNITIES
● To taste a variety of citrus fruits
● To create real juice
● To develop fine manipulation skills.

YOU WILL NEED
Four small plastic jugs; a large bowl; a sharp knife (for adult use only); three oranges; three lemons; three limes; a juicer; small plastic tumblers.

Real juice

Sharing the game
● Put all the fruits into a large bowl.
● Place the bowl of fruit on the floor so that your child can explore the contents.
● As she explores the variety of fruits use appropriate language to describe the colour, texture and scents.
● Take three of the jugs and place them beside you and your child.
● Choose two of the oranges and cut them in half.
● Squeeze the oranges in the juicer and pour the juice into one of the jugs. Make sure that your child can clearly see what you are doing.
● Repeat this with the lemons and then the limes, pouring the juice into the other jugs.
● Now pour a little of the orange juice into a cup and invite her to pour some into another. Repeat this with the lemon and lime juice.
● Taste and smell each of the juices. Which one does your child like the best?

● Now let your child mix her own choice of juices into the fourth jug. What shall we call this juice? What does it taste like?

Taking it further
● Provide your child with some paper and some green, yellow and orange crayons. Cut the paper into circles by drawing round a small plate.
● Look at the selection of fruit that remains in the bowl. Talk about the shapes and colours with your child. Ask her to use the crayons to draw pictures of the fruits. Let your child make marks freely on the page – it does not need to look anything like the real thing!

TASTE

AGE RANGE
2-3 years

LEARNING OPPORTUNITIES
● To become more familiar with a variety of fruits
● To develop hand-to-eye co-ordination and fine manipulation skills
● To create a healthy snack.

YOU WILL NEED
Two bananas; two large oranges; two kiwi fruit; strawberries; grapes; two peaches; two pears; plates; stiff straws; napkins; a knife.

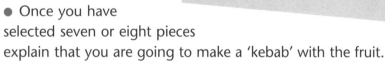

Fruit kebabs

Sharing the game
● Prepare each of the fruits – peeling, slicing and stoning them. While you do this, talk about what you are doing.
● Place the prepared fruit pieces on a few large plates. Ask your child to help.
● Ask him to tell you which fruits he likes and which fruits he doesn't like so much. Talk about the fruit, taking the lead from your child's awareness of colour, texture and so on.
● Ask him to select some of the pieces while you do the same. Place the pieces onto a plate of your own. While you select your pieces say, 'I will choose banana – it's nice and soft', or 'I'll take orange next as it's really juicy'.
● Once you have selected seven or eight pieces explain that you are going to make a 'kebab' with the fruit.
● Demonstrate by taking one of the straws and pushing your selected fruit pieces on.
● Your child will find this challenging and will need some help, so as not to end up with a squashy mess! If necessary, make some holes in the fruit for your child so that he only has to thread them on.

Taking it further
● Make a 'Knickerbocker Glory' with your child, placing the fruit pieces into a tall glass and spooning in some yoghurt or ice-cream.
● Make a cocktail – pour a little orange juice into a tall cup and choose some fruit to add. Invite your child to do the same. Drink your cocktail with straws and use a spoon to scoop out the fruity bits!

TASTE

AGE RANGE
2-3 years

LEARNING OPPORTUNITIES
● To taste a variety of breakfast cereals
● To develop pincer grip
● To develop vocabulary.

YOU WILL NEED
A selection of variety pack cereals; small ramekin dishes or small bowls; small and large spoons.

Cereal selection

Sharing the game
● Place all the small boxes of cereal on a low table.
● Sit with your child and look at the boxes. Does your child have a favourite one? Which one is it? What is it called and why does she like that one?

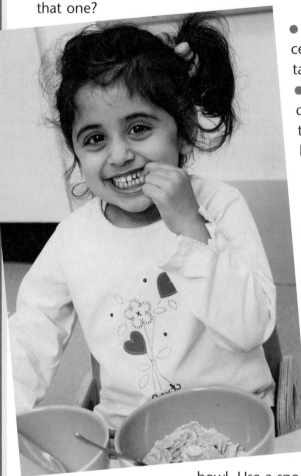

● Next, name each type of cereal, look at the writing and talk about the pictures.
● Invite her to select three different boxes and open them – she may need some help.
● Let her empty some of the contents from each box into the small bowls. Explore the contents, by taste, touch, smell and sight.
● Take turns to close your eyes and 'feed' each other a piece of cereal from one of the bowls. Can you and your child guess which type of cereal you are eating?
● Now make some combinations of cereal pieces in another small bowl. Use a spoon to stir them round. Comment on the different shapes and colours.

Taking it further
● Thread some hoop-shaped cereal pieces onto a straw or chopstick to develop fine motor skills.
● Give your child a sweet lace and invite her to thread some cereal pieces onto the lace. Make patterns and talk about the variety of shapes and colours. Let your child eat her necklace.

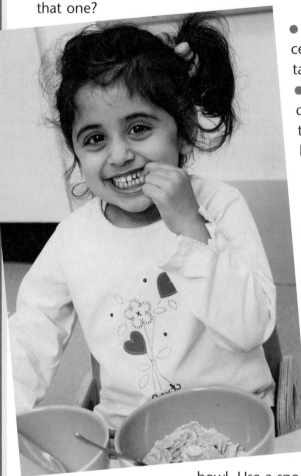

TASTE

AGE RANGE
2-3 years

LEARNING OPPORTUNITIES
● To taste a number of different crisps
● To encourage making choices.

YOU WILL NEED
Small bowls; a carrier bag; three or four varieties of crisps such as cheese puffs, salt and vinegar long maize snacks, cheese and onion square crisps, tortilla chips, pretzels, onion rings and prawn-flavoured snacks.

What crisp?

Sharing the game
● Place all the packets of crisps into a carrier bag.
● Sit down with your child and show him the bag. Tell him that you have put three or four different types of packets of crisps in this bag. Tell him the names of each type of crisp.
● Tell him that you would like him to put his hand in the bag and pull out a packet. Can he guess which packet he might pull out?
● Let him put his hand into the carrier bag without looking and slowly take a packet out. Can he tell you which one he has pulled out? Does he like this kind of crisp?
● Repeat this a few times.
● Then open the packets and empty each one into a separate bowl.
● Invite your child to choose a crisp. Talk about its shape, texture, smell and taste.
● Encourage your child to try each type. Are there any that he doesn't like?
● Provide him with a bowl of his own and suggest that he makes a snack selection by choosing a handful of his favourite crisps. Perhaps he would like to select some for you too.

Taking it further
● Use some of the crisps to create a picture. For example, a face with onion ring eyes, a cheese stick nose and a smiley cheese puff mouth!
● Keep the empty packets and use them to play shops. Add some tins and packets from your store cupboard and help your child to take turns with you to be the shopkeeper and customer.

TASTE

AGE RANGE
2-3 years

LEARNING OPPORTUNITIES
● To introduce some different types of bread
● To create sandwiches
● To develop spreading skills.

YOU WILL NEED
A selection of types of bread such as pitta bread, focaccia, naan, croissant, panini, unleavened bread, crusty bread, French bread, bagels; plates; butter knives; butter; cheese spread; cheese slices; cucumber; tomatoes; jam; cold meat.

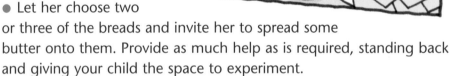

Sandwich time

Sharing the game
● Ask your child to help you wash the tomatoes and cucumber. Cut them into slices and put them onto some plates.
● Prepare the cheese and cold meat.
● Sit with your child and look at all the different kinds of bread. Talk about them and name them, perhaps telling them about where they are from or how they are made.
● Let her choose two or three of the breads and invite her to spread some butter onto them. Provide as much help as is required, standing back and giving your child the space to experiment.
● Explain that you would like her to make a sandwich by choosing something as a filling from the selection of food on the plates.
● Try to encourage your child to choose one or two things for her sandwich, so as not to overfill it! Explain that she can always make another sandwich after this one if she wants to.
● Let your child make and enjoy a range of small sandwiches. Talk about her preferences and feel and describe the different bread textures together.

Taking it further
● Make some bread together. Buy a bread mix from any supermarket and help your child to follow the instructions you give her.
● Make some garlic bread together. Cut slits in a stick of French bread and ask your child to stuff it with garlic butter (made from crushed garlic mixed with butter). Wrap in foil and bake in a moderate oven for about eight minutes. Enjoy it together!

CHAPTER 4

SMELL

From very early on in his life your baby will recognise familiar smells. This ability to recognise smells, coupled with his other senses, will help him to begin to understand what he is experiencing. You will soon notice that your baby turns his face away from unpleasant and sometimes unfamiliar smells. His sense of security when he is with and around familiar smells will help towards making him a happy, confident and content baby.

BONDING

The bonding process between you and your baby is hugely supported by his sense of smell. During the close contact of breastfeeding he will not only come to recognise the smell of your milk, but the scent of perfume or soap you have used. He will very quickly be able to recognise you and other main carers by their smell. If you are not breastfeeding be sure to hold your baby close to you so that he can smell your scent. Where possible, avoid placing him in a chair or pram to bottle feed, as you will lose an important opportunity to strengthen the bond between you. There are of course, other times when you will be holding your baby close to you and these too will strengthen the bonds between you and your baby.

How you can help

● During feeding and changing make close contact with your child. Try not to rush these routines. Make sure these processes are carried out in a calm and comfortable environment.
● Sing and whisper to your baby during intimate moments.
● Keep your baby close by as you wash and dress yourself, allowing him to enjoy the various aromas you use. Talk to him all the time, encouraging him to respond with babbling and cooing.
● If you are using soap or cream on your baby, express your delight in the scents as you use them.

Think first! Babies and young children have very sensitive skin and many have allergic reactions to soaps and chemicals. Baby and infantile eczema is a very common complaint and can be aggravated by close contact with perfumed products. If in doubt about a product's suitability then do not use it.

SHARING SCENTS AND AROMAS

Adults tend to take the smells we experience very much for granted. We are able to associate a certain smell with the item that emits it due to our experiences of the world. You can help your baby learn about smells with repetitive activities and routines, drawing his attention to the smells and their origins as you go about your daily lives.

For example, your day might start with the smell of soap and toothpaste, baby wipes and lotions, followed by the smell of coffee, toast and jam. As the day goes on you will encounter other smells. In fact, if you stop and think about your day in detail you will realise that there is a huge array of different smells that you can share with your child.

How you can help

● Each time you are using an item that has some kind of scent introduce it to your baby.

● As you are sharing a snack or preparing lunch, talk about the different smells. Call your child's attention to them as he eats.

● Try to find a balance between offering foods that smell familiar to your child and those that are new to them.

● When washing your baby try to use the same soap and cream – this will allow him to enjoy something he is familiar with.

● Allow your baby to smell the scents of fresh flowers. If you use an oil burner, use the same aromas so that he gets used to them and can recognise the scents.

SMELL ACTIVITIES

As adults, we often associate smells with particular memories – some we like, some we dislike. This will be the same for your child. Your child will learn more about nice and familiar smells as he is introduced to them. He will begin to recognise the smells and make associations with them as he meets them more often. Offer him a rich variety of activities that encourage him to enjoy the aromas of his environment. Place fresh flowers or pot plants around his environment so that he can experience the scents. Burn scented candles or oils to create pleasant aromas around the house. Bring your child close to the smells and talk about them with him to encourage the development of his vocabulary. Your child will eventually be able to express his opinions about certain smells, firstly through his expressions and body language and then through his speech and increasing vocabulary.

Think first! Make sure that you only have non-poisonous plants and flowers in places that he might come into contact with them. A short list of some of the more dangerous plants and flowers can be found in Dr Miriam Stoppard's *New Baby Care Book* (Dorling Kindersley).

How you can help

● Place small drops of perfume onto cotton wool balls and pop them into some plastic tumblers. Let your child smell the scents from a distance.

● Place a variety of spices into the toes of some baby socks, tie them off and let your baby smell them from a distance.

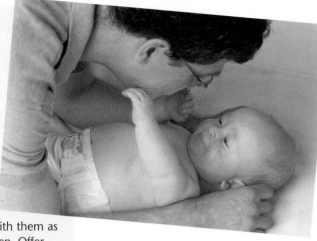

● Hang some dried flowers around your baby's changing station so that you can bring them to your baby and let him smell them before hanging them up again.

NEGATIVE RESPONSE

The more often the sense of smell is stimulated, the more it opens up the pathways to each part of the brain. Always be ready for a negative reaction – your baby may not like every scent you introduce him to. If he demonstrates dislike, withdraw the aroma. While exposing him to the scent of herbs and foodstuffs, explain what you are doing and name the items as you encourage him to enjoy the smells.

How you can help

● Avoid very strong, harsh smells.

● Always react with a positive facial expression and positive description of new smells.

● Scent smells make a deep impression on a child. There is often no barrier to their penetrating influence. For this reason it is important that we are aware of keeping areas clean, bright and fresh.

● Consider a variety of scents that promote calm, comfort and a secure homely atmosphere.

SMELL

AGE RANGE
0-1 year

LEARNING OPPORTUNITIES
● To appreciate different aromas
● To develop the sense of smell
● To develop hand-to-eye co-ordination.

YOU WILL NEED
Small linen bags; small baby socks; a lemon; a lime; a grapefruit; a pineapple; a banana; a strawberry; brightly-coloured thin ribbon.

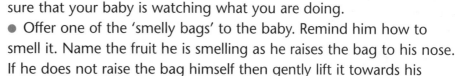

Lots of peel

Sharing the game
● Choose a range of fruits that you need to peel (see the ideas in the panel). Peel each one.
● Place the peel of each fruit into a separate linen/muslin bag or baby sock.
● Use the thin bright ribbon or a thin length of elastic to securely tie the top of each bag.
● Now raise one of your 'smelly' bags to your nose and sniff it, making

sure that your baby is watching what you are doing.
● Offer one of the 'smelly bags' to the baby. Remind him how to smell it. Name the fruit he is smelling as he raises the bag to his nose. If he does not raise the bag himself then gently lift it towards his nose. If he does not seem to want it, withdraw it.
● Take your baby's lead. Let him smell the same bag several times before offering him a new one. Watch as he touches the other bags.
● Encourage him to repeat the process, reminding him how to raise the bag and sniff the contents.
● Name and smell each bag that your baby chooses.
● Finish by smelling and then tasting some of the fruits together.

Taking it further
● Place scented tissues or fabric softener sheets in the bags.
● Put some pot pourri in the bags and let him smell the contents from a distance.
● Arrange the fruit in the basket and let him explore the textures and scents.

AGE RANGE
0-1 year

LEARNING OPPORTUNITIES
● To visually appreciate the outdoor environment
● To develop balance and co-ordination
● To enjoy the scents of herbs and flowers.

YOU WILL NEED
Access to a garden or park; large pots of herbs; flowers; heathers and so on.

Scented walk

Sharing the game
● Check out the outdoor area you are planning to visit. Make sure that the plants and herbs are accessible for your baby, whether she is toddling or in a pushchair.
● Depending on the season and weather, dress your baby accordingly.
● Sit your child in her pushchair (or hold her hand ready to toddle, depending on the stage your child has reached).
● Walk with, or push baby in her pushchair among the various plants. Stop at each one and gently pull the plant towards you both. If you are not able to approach the plants in this way pick a small piece of each herb and flower.
● Next, sit with baby on the grass or kneel beside the pushchair and explore the herbs together. Rub a little of the herb onto your own fingertips and offer your fingertips to your baby to smell. Talk about what you are doing and what you have found out yourself.

Taking it further
● Call your baby's attention to herbs and flowers while shopping together.
● Look at photos of flowers and pretend to smell them.
● Place a few silk flowers next to real ones and offer them both to your baby to smell.

SMELL

AGE RANGE
0-1 year

LEARNING OPPORTUNITIES
● To enjoy the sensations of water and other textures
● To enjoy a variety of scents.

YOU WILL NEED
A baby bath; water; cotton wool; a flannel; liquid soap (suitable for babies); baby shampoo; baby oil; baby lotion; a large soft towel.

Bath time

Sharing the game
● Pour some water into the baby bath. Sit beside it with your baby.
● Pour a small amount of baby's liquid soap into your palm and let him smell it with you.
● Smear a tiny amount onto his palm, rub it around and then wipe it with a flannel or some cotton wool.

● Do this again with a little baby shampoo, then baby bath, baby oil and baby lotion. Explain what you're doing.
● Repeat on baby's legs and tummy!
● Gently put your baby into the bath and wash and then dry him properly, calling attention to the various aromas throughout the experience.

Taking it further
● Use a baby wipe to clean your baby's hands. Call his attention to the smell.
● Snuggle your baby up into a soft towelling robe. Smell the scent of the washing powder and any other baby lotion or talcum powder smells that linger in the robe.
● Put a pea-sized amount of toothpaste onto your baby's brush and encourage him to smell it before he puts it into his mouth. Offer him some similar substances to smell, such as a peppermint sweet and peppermint oil products.

○○○○○○○○○○○○○○○○○○○○○○○○○○○○○○

SMELL

LEARNING OPPORTUNITIES
● To stimulate the sense of smell
● To introduce a wide range of scents
● To develop hand-to-eye co-ordination.

YOU WILL NEED
Some fabric swatches; small pieces of card; cotton wool pads or balls; flower petals; pot pourri; some fresh mint leaves; coffee granules; lavender; grated soap; bright ribbon or cord; a small basket or mat.

Scented sachets

Sharing the game
● Prepare a range of scented bags.
● Drip the scents onto cotton wool or place a small amount of the scent between two pieces of card.
● Create simple small bags with the fabric swatches by folding the pieces of fabric in half and either stitching or gluing the edges securely. Leave an opening at the top of each bag to place the scented card or cotton wool inside.
● Place a piece of scented cotton wool or a scented cardboard 'sandwich' into each bag. Tie the tops of the bags securely with the ribbon or cord, making sure that your baby cannot remove the contents from the bag.
● Place the bags in a small basket or on a mat on the floor.
● Sit with your baby, lifting the bags and smelling them. Offer her one to touch and encourage her to lift and smell the contents.

Taking it further
● Hide each bag under a cushion or favourite toy.
● Take her hand and walk (or carry her) around to find the hidden scents. Marvel at the treasures together when you find them!

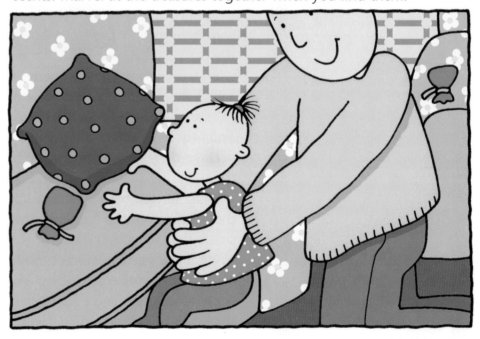

SMELL

AGE RANGE
1-2 years

LEARNING OPPORTUNITIES
● To taste and smell a variety of fruit
● To encourage choice making.

YOU WILL NEED
Strawberries; kiwi fruit; an apple; grapes; a banana; two small bowls; two large bowls; jug of water; kitchen roll; cutting board; knife.

Fruit salad

Sharing the game
● Place all the fruit into a large bowl.
● Place the kitchen roll on a low table or on the floor beside the bowl of fruit.
● Offer your baby a small bowl and take one yourself.
● Take the jug of water and invite your baby to help you pour it into the other large bowl. Explain that you will both be using this water to wash the fruit before you eat it.

● Talk about all the fruits that can be seen in the fruit bowl. Describe each fruit to your baby as you name it, commenting on the colour, size and shape of each type of fruit.
● Next, lift each piece up to smell it. Encourage your baby to smell it too.
● Wash the fruit and allow him to 'wash' a piece then place it into his small bowl. Suggest that you cut it and then do so. Ask him to smell it again. Offer it to him to eat.
● Repeat this with each fruit, using as wide a vocabulary as possible.
● Remember that your baby may prefer to watch and may not wish to taste all the fruits.

Taking it further
● Hide the cut fruits in a bowl of yoghurt or custard.
● Using a spoon, lift the fruit piece to your nose saying, 'Yum! Yum! What a delicious smell. This strawberry is so sweet!'.

AGE RANGE
1-2 years

LEARNING OPPORTUNITIES
● To develop fine motor control skills
● To develop pincer grip
● To introduce smell and texture.

YOU WILL NEED
Paper plates; a saucer; black sugar paper; a pencil; green toothpaste; blue toothpaste; pink and white striped toothpaste (children's toothpastes are preferable); scissors.

Just like snow!

Sharing the game
● Put a paper plate in between yourself and your toddler.
● Cut the black sugar paper into small circles (by drawing round a saucer).
● Place the tubes of toothpaste beside the paper plates.
● Take the lid off each one.
● Choose a tube and help the toddler to squeeze a little bit of it onto the paper plate. Suggest she pops her finger tip in and smells it. Talk about the smell with your toddler.

● Choose a black sugar paper circle and make a mark with the toothpaste. Suggest she does the same, if she is not attempting to already.
● Show your toddler how to use the toothpaste on the black paper to make a snowy scene!
● Repeat this with each of the toothpastes, calling attention to the different textures, colours and smells.

Taking it further
● Make a few small bowls of icing sugar. Add scents and flavourings. Use them to create a new 'snow scene' on the black sugar paper.
● Rub some of the 'snow' onto a small length of silver foil. Encourage your toddler to experience the different textures as well as the scents.

AGE RANGE
1-2 years

LEARNING OPPORTUNITIES
● To enjoy creating aromas
● To develop hand-to-eye co-ordination
● To make marks.

YOU WILL NEED
A basket; a bowl; sandpaper (different colours and textures); scented candles; soaps; cinnamon sticks; crayons; chalks and pastels; scissors.

Sandpaper art

Sharing the game
● Cut the sandpaper into different shapes and sizes.
● Place the sandpaper into the basket.
● Place the other items (which will be used as mark makers) into the bowl.
● Take one of the mark makers from the bowl, smell it and describe the scent to your toddler.
● Allow him to do the same, helping him if necessary. Use the opportunity to help your toddler to increase his vocabulary, by suggesting new words too.
● Now use your chosen mark makers to draw onto the pieces of sandpaper. Exclaim at the wonderful marks your toddler is creating!
● Continue to choose new mark makers from the selection available. Each time, comment on the colours, textures and scents.
● Together, smell the results of the mark making every now and then.
● Thread ribbons through the pieces of sandpaper and hang the 'art' in a window or doorway. As the wind passes through, the aromas should spread.

Taking it further
● Place a thin layer of loose sand on a shallow tray. Place some mark makers beside it and let your child experiment with the sand.
● Drip glue lines across a page, then shake a mixture of sand and baby talcum powder onto the lines to create a textured, scented sand picture.

SMELL

AGE RANGE
1-2 years

LEARNING OPPORTUNITIES
● To create small scented sachets
● To enjoy creating new scents
● To develop hand-to-eye co-ordination.

YOU WILL NEED
Fabric swatches; scissors; four bars of strong scented soap (such as apple, strawberry, tangerine, lemon); thin ribbon; grater or knife; plates; bowls.

Bags of scent

Sharing the game
● Cut out some large circles from the fabric.
● Invite your toddler to choose one of the soap bars. Smell it together.
● Explain that you are going to grate it. Let her watch what is happening.
● Place the grated soap into a bowl.
● Repeat this with each of the soaps, each time enjoying the aroma.
● Show your toddler how to choose some soap 'shards' and place them on one of the fabric circles. Tie up the circle with a thin piece of ribbon to make a little scented bag.
● Encourage your toddler to make several bags in the same way, helping her to tie the bags securely. Which soap does your toddler like the smell of best?
● Hang the scented bags around your toddler's environment, in places such as around her changing mat, on her bedroom door and so on. Do not place them near or within reach of your toddler's bed or cot as they may present a choking risk.
● Squeeze the bags each time you are nearby and enjoy the scents together.

Taking it further
● Use fruit peel instead of soap. The bright colours and vibrant scents will be very stimulating.
● Place a variety of fresh herbs in bags and enjoy the aromas.

SMELL

AGE RANGE
1-2 years

LEARNING OPPORTUNITIES
● To encourage fine manipulation
● To encourage creation of a scented picture.

YOU WILL NEED
Shallow trays; white paper; two or three scented liquid soaps in dispenser bottles; empty sauce bottles.

Soap trail

Sharing the game
● Place the soaps onto a low surface.
● Squirt a small amount of each into the palm of your hand. Let your toddler smell the soaps.
● Ask if he would like to make a picture with the soaps.
● Place a piece of paper onto each tray, one for you and one for your toddler.
● Pour some of the soap into the clean squeezy sauce bottles.
● Choose one of

the soaps and explain that you are going to make a soap picture. Show your toddler how to squeeze a small amount of soap in swirly and creative patterns onto your piece of paper. It does not matter if the colours merge into each other and don't worry if they also seep into the paper. With this activity it is the sensation of squeezing and the wonderful scents that your toddler will enjoy that are the most important things.
● Invite your toddler to do this carefully with each of the soaps. He may need some help to control the flow!
● Enjoy the scents of your soapy pictures.

Taking it further
● Pour a shallow amount of water into a washing up bowl. Squirt some of the liquid soap into the water and create bubbles with a whisk. Draw your child's attention to the smell of the soapy bubbles.

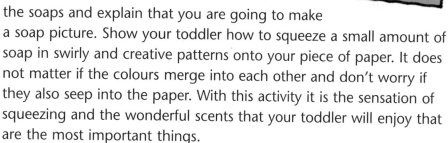

SMELL

AGE RANGE
2-3 years

LEARNING OPPORTUNITIES
● To introduce the scents of herbs
● To explore the living environment
● To appreciate the natural world.

YOU WILL NEED
Fresh herbs such as mint; marjoram; fennel; parsley; thyme and sage as well as bottles of each type of herb (in dried form) to compare; small bowls.

THINK FIRST!
Make sure that your toddler understands that she must not pick, eat or smell plants and flowers in the house and garden unless you are with her and say that it is all right to do so. Explain that some plants might be poisonous.

Herb pots

Sharing the game
● If possible plant some herbs with your toddler. Choose and prepare a patch in your garden or plant them in pots. Make sure that she washes her hands carefully after handling the soil.
● Alternatively buy the herbs on the list above, either in small pots or freshly cut in packets.
● Place the gathered herbs in some small bowls, one type per bowl.
● Sit with your toddler and smell the contents of each bowl of fresh herbs.
● Now place a little of each bottled dried herb into its own separate small bowl and smell these.
● Now revisit the bowls of fresh herbs. Show your child how to pick up one of the leaves and rub it gently between her fingertips to release the aroma. Smell the scents. Do the smells remind her of any of the smells from the bowls of dried herbs?
● Together, try to match up some of the fresh and dried herb scents. Some will be more obvious than others.

Taking it further
● Use some of the herbs she has helped to pick to make herb bread. Make slits in a stick of French bread and add a mixture of butter and chopped fresh herbs. Wrap the bread in aluminium foil and bake in a moderate oven for about eight minutes until the butter has melted into the bread.

LEARNING OPPORTUNITIES
● To introduce flower names
● To enjoy creating an arrangement of flowers
● To enjoy the scent of various flowers.

YOU WILL NEED
Two or three small pieces of oasis and one large piece; tulips; daffodils; irises; carnations; a large basket.

Flower power

Sharing the game
● Cut the flowers from your garden or separate the chosen ones from a bunch you have bought.
● Place the flowers into a large basket.
● Sit with your toddler and encourage him to look at and explore the variety of flowers in the basket.
● While he is exploring, describe the flower he is holding or looking at, by colour, shape and name.
● Encourage him to smell each of the flowers. Which flower smells the best?
● Set challenges, such as choosing a flower from the basket and asking him to choose another one the same.
● Offer your child a small piece of oasis and take one for yourself.
● Choose two or three flowers and manipulate them into the oasis.
● Create a few pre-prepared holes in your toddler's oasis to help him push in his choice of flowers.
● Next take the larger oasis and use the rest of the flowers to create a beautiful arrangement together.

Taking it further
● Suggest he chooses a place to display his flowers.
● Let him pick some flowers from the garden or a flower pot to place in a small vase or bowl and again choose a place for it to be displayed. Emphasise that he must only pick flowers from the garden when you say it is alright to do so. Make sure that he realises he must never take flowers from wild places, or other gardens. Show him daisies and dandelions and explain that it is alright to pick these.

LEARNING OPPORTUNITIES
● To be stimulated by a wide variety of spices
● To make a multi-sensory picture.

YOU WILL NEED
Sticky-backed plastic; wallpaper lining; water; large paint brush or roller; variety of spice and herb pots with sprinkle lids such as paprika, garlic, cinnamon, mild curry powder, five spice, rosemary and thyme.

Spice sprinkle

Sharing the game
● Look at the spice bottles together. Explain that some strong smelling spices are inside the bottles.
● Invite your toddler to sprinkle a little of each of the spices (one by one) onto the palm of your hand.
● Smell the scent and then allow her to. Hold it far enough away so that it is not too strong and so that your child does not inhale it.
● Repeat this with a few of the different spices.
● Explain that you are going to make a picture with the spices. Invite her to join in and help you.
● Take a paint brush or roller each. Dip it into the water and spread it on a length of lining paper.
● Once the paper has been covered in water, invite her to sprinkle the spices with you, creating a spicy picture.

Taking it further
● Add some glitter or powdered paint to the spices.
● Instead of water, brush a thin layer of glue and make a multi-scented collage by sticking herbs, spices, petals and sequins to the paper. Cover with sticky-backed plastic.

SMELL

AGE RANGE
2-3 years

LEARNING OPPORTUNITIES
● To explore the fingers and hands
● To develop small muscles
● To strengthen the bonds between yourself and your toddler.

YOU WILL NEED
A range of oils that are safe to use with babies and young children (Mothercare, Boots or Avent are good sources of such products); baby wipes; soft towels; small bowls.

Palm rub

Sharing the game
● Cuddle your toddler, tickle him under the chin, on the tummy and behind the ears.
● Play hand games together saying rhymes such as 'Round and Round the Garden' (on the photocopiable sheet on page 128).
● Look in *This Little Puffin*, compiled by Elizabeth Matterson (Puffin) for some further suggestions for 'tickly' or action rhymes.

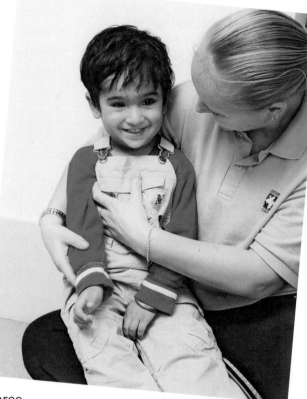

● Pour a little of the scented baby oils into three bowls. Add some peppermint essence to the fourth bowl.
● Choose one of the oils and rub it into your palm. Suggest that your child does so too (either in your hand or his own).
● Smell the palm of you hand, then choose a different fragrance. This time use your fingertips to rub the oil along your arm. Suggest that your child does the same.
● Let your child experiment with the different oils and fragrances. When you feel that he is ready to finish, offer him a baby wipe to wipe his hands with. Wipe your own at the same time.
● Finish by washing your hands together, using the soft towels to dry them.

Taking it further
● Instead of oil use a liquid soap. Watch the soap turn to bubbles as you get your hands wet. Draw your child's attention to the different feel and smell of the soap compared to the oil.

SMELL

AGE RANGE
2-3 years

LEARNING OPPORTUNITIES
● To introduce a variety of strong smells
● To encourage an appreciation of taste.

YOU WILL NEED
Small empty plastic bottles that you can't see through; coffee; kettle; peppermint cordial; water; cups; fresh limes and lemons; juicer; spoons.

Which drink?

Sharing the game
● Wash out the plastic bottles. Let your child help. Rinse them thoroughly, ensuring that no residue is left.
● Make a weak cup of coffee and let it cool down. Pour the cold coffee into one of the bottles. Invite your child to smell the contents of the bottle. Does she know what the smell is?
● Invite your child to help you mix some peppermint cordial and water. Pour the mixture into a second bottle.
● Cut the lemons and limes in half and then squeeze them on the juicer. Talk to your child about what is happening. Help your child to pour the juice you have made into another bottle. Talk about the delicious smell together as she pours it in.
● Encourage your child to put the lids onto each of the bottles. Check that the lids are secure.
● Invite her to shake each of the bottles.
● Now ask her to open the bottles, one at a time, and challenge her to identify the smells.

● Pour a small amount onto a saucer to see if your child guessed correctly from the smell alone. Emphasize that it doesn't matter if she was right or wrong. Does the colour of the mixture provide any more clues?

Taking it further
● Make the same drinks again. This time, make them weak enough to taste (by adding extra water) and invite your child to taste the drinks as well as smell them.

CHAPTER 5

SIGHT

As well as the senses of touch, taste and smell, sight plays an important role in the initial stages of the development of your relationship with your child.
Even babies of a few months react to a bright light, colourful mobile or a patterned blouse. They are attracted to a wide variety of visual stimuli and quite often it is the most natural and easy way to engage with your baby.

THE LIVING SPACE
By providing an interesting and colourful environment you will be helping your baby to learn and develop. It is, of course, the way that you share your baby's visual experiences that is of the most importance. Talking about what your child can see and introducing him to new objects and images will help his development more than any colourful toy alone. Care must be taken not to overload your baby, as he can quickly become overstimulated.

How you can help
● Ensure that his play space, sleeping space and eating space are visually interesting and attractive.
● Avoid clutter and too many toys in your child's play space. Young children find it hard to focus their attention if there is too much on offer.
● Create a quiet, calm atmosphere in your child's sleeping space with soft lighting and spaces to rest their eyes on.
● Make your child's eating space bright and inviting. Avoid the temptation of having a television constantly on and try not to distract your child with too many toys. Use bright interesting utensils and allow your child to bring a comfort toy if you feel he needs it.

EYE CONTACT
It is very important to make eye-to-eye contact with your baby as you talk to, tickle, change and feed him. This allows your baby to focus and concentrate on your face, picking up all of your features and voice.

How you can help
● Sit close to your baby while talking to her. Encourage him to focus on your face if you want him to listen.
● Play peek-a-boo games taking eye contact away and then bringing it back.

OFFERING VISUAL STIMULI
While your baby is not mobile he will rely on you to introduce things for him to look at. He will be eager to look for and find things he drops. His natural curiosity will make him look under, over, in and around new toys or other items he encounters.

Use trays, baskets and boxes to gather a variety of familiar and unusual items for him to explore. Encourage him to look carefully at the things he is holding or to take a closer look at things he spots at a distance.

How you can help
● While playing together bring a wide variety of items from around the home for him to look at closely.
● Introduce him to his teddies and toys, encouraging him to take notice of his playthings.
● Call attention to the textures and patterns on his clothes.

FOLLOW HIS INTERESTS
Follow your baby's gaze and see what he finds interesting. Encourage him to explore with all his senses, helping him to understand that he can gather more information from touching and lifting something rather than just looking.

How you can help
● Notice what your child is gazing at, then bring it closer so that he can explore it.
● Offer unusual items from around the room for him to look at.
● Look at magazines together, pointing out interesting pictures.

LOOK BUT DON'T TOUCH
It is hard for your baby or toddler to understand that some things must only be looked at and not touched, due to safety or other reasons. It is an important skill for your young child to master, particularly with relation to not touching hot or sharp objects. To encourage this self-discipline you may choose to place a favourite object out of reach but within sight of your child. Help him to appreciate the pleasure of just looking at a pretty object. Be patient as this is a skill that needs a lot of practice.

How you can help
● When out with your child, stop at shop windows and draw his attention to interesting items.
● Take your child into art galleries and museums and call his attention to the various exhibits. Choose your visit carefully, making sure that the artwork and exhibits will hold your child's attention.

THE ENVIRONMENT
Inviting your child to look closely at his environment will enable him to become familiar with where things are kept and what is available to him. Consider what he can see from his cot or bouncy chair. What does he see from his changing mat? Place a variety of interesting objects near his cot, changing these regularly to visually excite and interest.

How you can help
● Introduce him to any pictures, alphabet friezes or mobiles in his room. Name and describe each wall hanging.
● Open cupboards and let him look inside. Let him see what is inside his chest of drawers.
● Lift him so that he can look out of his window – in fact let him look out of every window at the different views around his home.

Think first! Make sure that all your windows and doors have secure window locks fitted.

LOOKING AT DETAIL
Looking in detail at things will eventually help your child's understanding of abstract concepts such as colour, texture and shape. He may not understand these until after his third birthday but it is important to encourage his visual awareness as often as possible.

The visual environment should reflect an interesting space, which encourages even the youngest child to explore the patterns, shapes and colours they are introduced to.

How you can help
● Change the pictures around your child's room from time to time. Don't change everything at once, but challenge him to notice what's new or gone.
● Hang any items you make or draw together on the wall.
● Put up family photographs for your child to look at and enjoy.

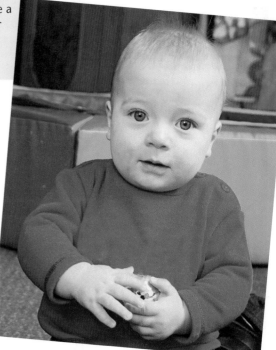

LEARNING OPPORTUNITIES
● To develop hand-to-eye co-ordination
● To encourage visual focus
● To foster a sense of curiosity.

YOU WILL NEED
Four empty shoe boxes; black and white paper; paint; pens; scissors; bright cord; large beads; a few small toys; sticky tape; glue.

Behind the door

Sharing the game

● Take the shoe boxes and cover two with black paper and two with white paper. Alternatively, mix some black and white paint with glue and paint two boxes in each colour.

● Using black on white and white on black, create bold patterns on each of the boxes. Cut out circles, stripes or squares and glue them on. Babies are visually attracted to striking contrasts from an early age and it is believed that by encouraging them to focus on contrasting patterns you will help to develop their concentration and visual perception skills.

● Using the scissors cut a reasonably large 'door' in each of the boxes. A different shape in each would be great.

● Make a door handle by threading some large beads onto a length of cord. Make two threading holes in the door and loop the cord through the holes tying the ends at the back.

● Place a bright, attractive toy in each box.

● Place the boxes on the floor and sit next to them with your baby.

● Open one of the 'doors' and exclaim at what you see. Close it again and slide the box nearer to your baby to see if he copies.

● Encourage him to take out the toy.

Taking it further

● Place a small snack wrapped in a napkin in each box. Repeat the game, enjoying the snacks.

● Hide some everyday items belonging to your baby inside the boxes. Ideas include his hat, his socks, and his brush.

AGE RANGE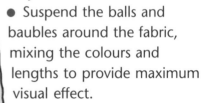
0-1 year

LEARNING OPPORTUNITIES
● To encourage scanning and focus of attention
● To stimulate visual response
● To create a bright and interesting environment.

YOU WILL NEED
Six or seven glitter balls and baubles; a variety of reflective colour baubles; bright ribbons; tinsel; sticky tape; drawing pins; a torch; a length of shiny fabric.

THINK FIRST!
Do not flash the light or make violent movements.

Glitter ball

Sharing the game
● Attach different lengths of brightly-coloured ribbon to each of the balls and baubles.
● Drape the shiny fabric in an attractive way on the ceiling above your child's changing station, cot or bouncy chair.
● Suspend the balls and baubles around the fabric, mixing the colours and lengths to provide maximum visual effect.
● Lie or sit underneath with your child and draw her attention to the various colours, types of fabric and so on. Talk about any movement that you can see. Do the balls spin round slowly in any breeze?
● Now use your torch to bounce light onto the fabric. Then shine it on the different baubles, talking about the shapes, colours and reflections you can see as you go.
● Finally, shine the light around slowly in a circle, then zig-zag between the objects.

Taking it further
● Hang ribbon and tinsel between the baubles and glitter balls.
● Hang a variety of your baby's favourite toys between the various items on the ceiling.
● Drape bright and shiny fabric swatches around the floor and over cushions for your baby to touch or crawl over.
● Hang a sheet of holographic wrapping paper on the wall at sitting height for her to explore.

LEARNING OPPORTUNITIES

● To stimulate the sense of sight
● To introduce a variety of lights
● To enjoy finding out about light.

YOU WILL NEED

A selection of lamps, lights and torches – fairy lights; lava lamps; bubble lamps; table lamps; angle-poised lamps; pencil torches; a large spotlight; a large torch; a small tent; a large piece of dark fabric to drape over the tent.

THINK FIRST!

Never leave your child unattended near to lamps they can reach. Take special care with lava and bubble lamps. Also be sensitive to the fact that some children are afraid of the dark and may not like to experiment with lights inside a tent. Be aware of any medical conditions such as epilepsy that may be affected by moving and flickering lights.

Light fantastic

Sharing the game

● Place a variety of the lamps around the room. Take your child on a lamplight tour to see them all.
● Choose a particularly interesting light, such as a lava or bubble lamp and focus your child's attention on it. Sit with your child and draw his attention to the patterns in the lava lamp or encourage him to follow the bubbles rising and falling in the bubble lamp.

● Hang fairy lights around the changing mat or cot. Ensure your child cannot reach them, but can stretch towards them.
● Finally, place a few lamps around the outside of a small tent. Go inside the tent and look back out together at the 'outside lights'.
● Drape some dark material over the tent and sit inside it together. 'Dance' the various torches around the tent. Give your child a torch to hold and encourage him to join in.

Taking it further

● Use different coloured scarves, gels and materials to drape over the end of the torches. Talk about the different lighting effects you have created.

SIGHT

AGE RANGE
0-1 year

LEARNING OPPORTUNITIES
● To stimulate visual awareness
● To develop listening and concentration skills
● To develop vocabulary.

YOU WILL NEED
Old food magazines (many supermarkets have free leaflets and magazines); scissors; plastic wallets; fruit; vegetables; glue stick; white paper.

Picture this

Sharing the game
● Choose a variety of food photographs from the magazines – the clearer the photograph the better. Foods that your baby may recognise would be ideal.
● Cut out the pictures, sticking each one onto a piece of white paper. This will make them more pleasing to look at and so will be more likely to catch your baby's visual attention.
● Place each of the mounted photographs into a plastic wallet (such as a freezer bag). Make sure that there is no writing covering the pictures.
● Sit on a mat with your baby and show her each photograph one at a time. Talk about it. Name the food and make a positive comment about it, talk about eating it.
● Repeat this with a few of the pictures. Stop when you get to a photograph that you have a real version of, such as a piece of fruit or a vegetable.

● Exclaim, 'Oh, an apple. I have got one of those!'. Give the apple to your baby to hold. Look at both the picture and the real object together. Name it again.
● Repeat this with a few pieces of real foods. Cut up one of the appropriate foods and let your baby taste it.

Taking it further
● Include a few photographs of toys or people in your collection. When you come to these pictures exclaim, 'Oh I can't eat that/her!'.
● Position the photographs around a clear space. Encourage her to move around in her own way to find the banana, ice-cream and so on.

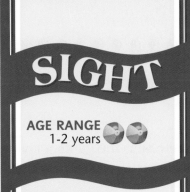

LEARNING OPPORTUNITIES
● To encourage small muscle development and pincer grip
● To develop an awareness of colour
● To encourage patience.

YOU WILL NEED
Five or six colours of crêpe or tissue paper (do not use non-run, you need it to run); lining paper or white porous paper; water squirter bottle; basket.

Colour squirt

Sharing the game
● Place the lengths of crêpe or sheets of tissue paper on the floor. Place the basket beside them.
● Sit with your child and explain to her that together you will gently rip the paper and place the small pieces into the basket. Don't make the pieces too small.
● When you have a basket full, rummage through them together. Explain that you are going to choose a few pieces and suggest she does this too.

● As you choose your pieces of paper, name each colour – this may prompt her to try to name the ones she selects.
● Place your pieces onto the large white paper and suggest she does so too, it doesn't matter where she puts them exactly.
● Take the bottle of water and squirt a few pieces of your torn paper. Give her the bottle and let her have a turn to squirt! Once the crêpe pieces are soaked you should notice the colour beginning to 'bleed'.
● Tell her that you are going to go away from the paper for a while and that you will check on it later.
● Do something else together.
● Return and then remove a few pieces of the paper. Look at the patterns it has made.
● Once more, go and do something else and repeat the process several times until all the paper pieces are removed.

Taking it further
● Use some of the removed tissue pieces to create a collage picture.
● Use a black felt-tipped pen to make some marks around the soft colour you have already created.

LEARNING OPPORTUNITIES
● To explore an object and introduce change
● To create an eye-catching interest area.

YOU WILL NEED
A large plant, small branch or dry twig arrangement; ribbons; tinsel; pictures; cards; crêpe paper; chains; a length of bright fabric; large vase or pot.

Decorating delights

Sharing the game
● Place the plant or small branch on the floor or in the garden. If you are arranging dry twigs help your child to place them carefully into the vase or pot.
● Ask him to help you gather the rest of the items needed from around the house. You may find it easier to place them where they are easy to find or reach before you begin.

● Choose an item each from those that you have gathered together, and place it on the branch or plant. Change its position a few times, making a show of deciding where it looks best.
● Repeat this with the various items. As he chooses each one, name it and guess where he'll place it, making it into a game.
● Suggest you go to find some more items to use for decoration.
● Once you have put the final decorating touches to your branch, plant or twigs, roll out the fabric. Look at it together and decide where it might look best.

Taking it further
● Create a small 'art gallery' beside the area you have created together. You might include photographs of your child and his family and friends, or you might include various pictures that he has made. Let him help by handing them to you and encourage him to decide where to position them.
● Look at some pictures of festivals and celebrations where trees and houses are decorated.

SIGHT

AGE RANGE
2-3 years

LEARNING OPPORTUNITIES
● To visually identify a range of pictures
● To explore photographs to gather information
● To develop oral communication.

YOU WILL NEED
Magazines (toy catalogues, shop promotional brochures); scissors; glue; A4 card.

Look at this

Sharing the game
● Gather a range of magazines. Look for photographs of children interacting with something, attempting to put on clothes, looking at shoes, painting and so on.
● Cut out some of the photographs from the magazines. Choose images that are clear without too much distracting detail.
● Include some photographs that show children in the context of their environment, such as a girl flying a kite at the top of a hill.
● Glue each of the photographs separately to a sheet of card.
● Invite your child to look through the photographs with you. Let her lead the description and affirm what she is saying as she describes what she sees.
● Choose a small selection and spread them on the floor.
● Point to one of the photographs and exclaim 'That's a nice blue ball', or 'Look, he's painting a picture!'.
● Challenge your child to point to the girl with the long hair, or the child who is holding a kite.

Taking it further
● Take photographs of your child carrying out routines, such as brushing her hair, washing her face, putting on her coat. Look at them together and talk about them.
● Look at picture books with hidden items and challenge her to find small items in the illustrations.
● Look at photographs of family snaps, holiday snaps or those taken on a day out. Create a small family album for her to look at.

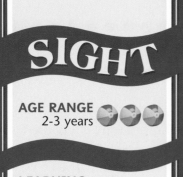

SIGHT

AGE RANGE
2-3 years

LEARNING OPPORTUNITIES
● To identify facial features
● To explore and describe a range of faces.

YOU WILL NEED
Five photos of your child (close up of head and shoulders); head and shoulders photos of grandparents, aunts and uncles, celebrities and babies; ribbon; Blu-Tack; a photocopier; paper.

Faces wall hanging

Sharing the game
● Select some photos of your child – try to vary the range of expressions on your child's face if possible.
● Gather other pictures from magazines or family – they do not need to be flattering!
● Gather some other photographs showing a range of hair styles, clothing, jewellery and so on! Include photographs that show people from a range of different cultures.
● Look at all the photographs together, talk about all the different types of people, clothing and so on. Make a selection of your favourite ones.

● Enlarge your chosen favourites to A4 size on a photocopier.
● Use Blu-Tack to hang them at your child's eye level, such as at the end of his bed, on an area of wall or around his toy box.
● Discuss the chosen photographs, calling his attention to various details. Has he chosen photographs of people that he knows? Are the people all different sizes and ages? What can he tell you about them?

Taking it further
● Choose six of the photographs and look at them together. Place them face down on the floor while your child watches. Can he find 'granny', his brother and so on?
● Let your child choose where to hang up his favourites. Help him to fix the photographs to his chosen places (children under three should not be allowed to handle Blu-Tack). Suggest two or three appropriate places for him to choose between.

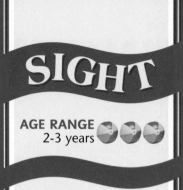

SIGHT

LEARNING OPPORTUNITIES
● To develop fine motor skills
● To develop hand-to-eye co-ordination
● To encourage independent use of scissors.

YOU WILL NEED
Bright material; holographic wrapping paper; tissue paper; aluminium foil; greaseproof paper; textured gift wrap; felt offcuts; fabric scraps; scissors; glue; large sheets of white paper; small bowls or plates; glue brush/spreader.

Patchwork picture

Sharing the game
● Place the various materials and papers on the floor, explore them together.
● Draw your child's attention to the textures, patterns and colours of the materials. Do any of them make a sound when touched, rubbed or shaken?
● Suggest you cut the materials using the scissors. Remind your child of the need to handle scissors carefully. Demonstrate how to use and handle them yourself.

● Offer her the easiest paper to cut and help her to position her fingers correctly in order to manipulate the scissors. She may wish to start by using two hands. Over time you will notice that this changes as her grip and manipulative skills develop.
● Cut different lengths, shapes and sizes of the different materials. Talk together about the ease or comparative difficulty of cutting the various types of paper and material.
● Explain to your child that she can use her cut pieces of material and paper to make a picture. Refer to the pieces as tiles and show her how to position them next to each other in attractive patterns.
● Give your child some glue and a spreader and allow her to experiment with the paper and material pieces to make an attractive picture on the white paper. It does not matter how she chooses to arrange her pieces.
● Praise your child for all her careful cutting and gluing work!

Taking it further
● Once the picture has dried suggest that your child might like to draw round or over some of the paper shapes with a pen or crayon.

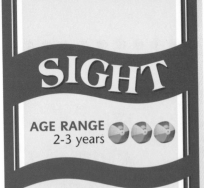

SIGHT

AGE RANGE
2-3 years

LEARNING OPPORTUNITIES
● To encourage recognition
● To develop a sense of curiosity
● To develop hand-to-eye co-ordination.

YOU WILL NEED
Animal pictures or photographs (such as those in a safari holiday brochure); large sheets of corrugated card; scissors; ribbons; glue.

Who's hiding?

Sharing the game
● Look at your selection of animal pictures and photographs with your child. Does he know the names of all the animals? Which ones are his favourites?

● Select photographs or pictures of five or six animals that your child will recognise.

● Use a piece of card and cut out some window flaps for the animals to hide behind. You will need to make the windows the right shape and size to reveal the animal that will be underneath.

● Then glue the pictures onto another large sheet of card, making sure that they are in the right places to be behind the windows you have cut out of the first piece of card.

● Attach small loops of ribbon to the window flaps to make handles that are easy for your child to manipulate.

● Attach the window sheet onto the animal sheet by gluing around the edges and pressing down firmly onto the card below. Double check to make sure you have lined the windows up carefully above the animal pictures.

● Sit with your child and encourage him to lift one of the windows. Challenge him to identify the animal he has found.

● Next, tap one of the windows and ask you child 'Who do you think is hiding?'.

● Repeat this with various windows, encouraging him to respond by making the sound of the hiding animal.

Taking it further
● Pretend to be various animals, making their sounds. Encourage your child to join in.

● Move around the room pretending to be the various animals – stomp like an elephant, stalk like a tiger, jump like a monkey.

CHAPTER 6

HEARING

Scientists would suggest that even before birth each one of us has an awareness of our surroundings through our senses, one of which is auditory awareness.

One of the most comforting sounds to your newborn baby is your voice and other familiar voices. As well as being able to identify voices, your child will quickly identify the sounds of his routines and his environment.

VERBAL COMMUNICATION
Verbal communication is a very important part of the bonding process. Face to face contact alongside a quiet gentle voice will offer comfort and security to your child. The more you talk to your child, the more he will recognise your voice. He will focus attention on the tone you use and will concentrate on the words he hears. The more words your child hears, the more words he will soon understand and learn.

How you can help
● Sit close to your child and talk gently, anything from rhymes and poems to general chatter.
● Sit opposite him and talk to him about the things he is wearing or sitting near.
● Repeat sounds around him and make musical sounds to accompany tunes,

such as, 'la, la, la'; 'doh, doh, doh'; and 'de-dum,de-dum,de-dum'!
● Make up silly tunes and encourage him to listen. When talking to your child, avoid confusing background sounds or music.
● Whenever possible, use real words – dog rather than doggy, train rather than 'choo, choo'.

CONCENTRATED LISTENING
Try to avoid having the television or radio on when you are talking to your child. Change the tone of your voice when you are talking to your child, using low and high pitches as appropriate. If you are happy and enthusiastic then highlight the emotion in your voice.

Encouraging your child to listen to gentle calming music at appropriate times, such as bathing or feeding is also beneficial. This will encourage your child to listen and concentrate. Introduce some movements that your baby can take part in with you as you listen to music, stimulating a response to the sounds.

How you can help
● Sit him on your knee and tap your toes to the beat of the music, changing to tapping him gently on his knee.
● Offer a variety of items, which will make sounds as he manipulates them. Introduce items from around the house that make sounds, such as a music box, telephone and clock.
● Use toys and objects that relate to words in the songs you sing.

MAKING YOUR OWN MUSIC

As well as the sounds he can hear as he manipulates objects, there are a rich variety of sounds he can make using his hands and feet. Encourage him to shake, tap, and squeeze toys and objects to create a range of sounds using his hands. Then encourage him to tip toe, stamp and clap using his feet and hands to create sounds.

How you can help

● Place a variety of objects in a basket that can be taped together to make a noise.

● Place different types of paper in a large bowl. Rip the different pieces to create a range of noises.

● Offer a range of materials – metal, wooden, plastic and cloth so that he can hear the different sounds that can be made when using them.

Think first! When encouraging your child to tap gently make sure that there is nothing breakable in sight!

SOUNDS ALL AROUND

We take for granted our ability to recognise all the sounds that we hear around us. Young children

too may be aware of them, but will not necessarily know what is causing them unless we take the time to show them. Encourage your child to listen to sounds – to the water running, the kettle boiling, the toaster popping, and so on. Hearing is essential in supporting your child's ability to concentrate and pay attention.

How you can help

● Involve him in what you do. If you create a sound, call his attention to it. Repeat the sound a few times – each time pretend to be listening closely and then act surprised when the sound is made!

● When outside, call attention to the sounds that your shoes make on the path, the grass and the pebbles. Encourage him to make the sounds too.

● Use a plant pot to drop items into, such as a leaf, a twig and a stone. Encourage him to hear the different sounds.

REPEATING SOUNDS

Be aware that all young children are different in what they like and dislike and they will respond differently to sounds. Whereas one child may enjoy lively, loud singing and stories, another may prefer a calmer and quieter approach.

Using songs and stories to repeat sounds is great fun. A story about a farm will allow you to create a tractor and animal noises over and over again! This will not only encourage your child to listen, but will also encourage him to make the sounds himself.

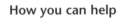

How you can help

● Sing the same few songs over and over again each day, giving your child the confidence to join in.

● Repeat sounds around the house, such as closing a door, running the taps and stirring your tea. Call attention to the sounds.

MUSIC AND MOVEMENT

Music and movement can have a calming effect. A restless baby or child may often be soothed by singing and dancing activities.

Young children enjoy listening to a wide range of songs and music, not just children's tunes. They will eagerly sway and dance around to music if you join in.

How you can help

● Listen to a short extract of music together, then repeat it – this time with movements.

● Play fast and slow music and vary the movements to reflect the tone.

● Play short bursts of music, dancing until the music stops, then listening and moving again when the music begins.

● Enjoy the sounds around you together. Help your child to use his sense of hearing to make sense of his environment.

LEARNING OPPORTUNITIES
● To aid muscular development
● To create and listen to a variety of sounds
● To develop an awareness of texture.

YOU WILL NEED
A plastic washing-up bowl; a metal bowl; a wooden box or bowl; cotton wool balls; pasta shapes; tin foil; wooden spoon; metal spoon; plastic spoon.

Stir round

Sharing the game
● Place the three empty bowls on the floor next to your baby.
● Place the three spoons next to the bowls.
● Encourage him to explore the various sounds he can make with the spoons and the bowls (stirring, tapping and so on).
● Tap one of the bowls lightly and ask him to do it too. Then make a show of banging the bowls to create a louder noise.
● Start by tapping once, then progress to several taps. Suggest that your baby experiments too.
● Next, show your baby how to stir round the bowls and encourage him to do the same.
● Invite your baby to help you to fill one of the bowls with the cotton wool balls. Explore the sound it makes when manipulated by the spoons.
● Repeat the game with the uncooked pasta and then lengths of tin foil.
● Mix the contents of the bowls with the spoons. Draw your baby's attention to the range of different sounds that are being created, using words such as soft, loud, noisy and quiet.

Taking it further
● Introduce a few different bowls and spoons.
● Add some different ingredients to the bowls, such as shredded paper, or silk flowers.

HEARING

AGE RANGE
0-1 year

LEARNING OPPORTUNITIES
● To create a range of verbal sounds
● To relate facial expressions to noises
● To encourage verbal response.

YOU WILL NEED
A comfortable area; some soft toys.

What a noise!

Sharing the game
● Sit opposite your baby. If possible, sit her at a height where she is in line with your face.
● Trace your finger down your cheek. Do the same with her cheeks. She may wish to do the same back to you. Encourage her to be gentle.
● Repeat with noses, chins and lips.
● Use your mouth to create sounds like that of a monkey, 'Ooh! Ooh! Ooh!'.
● Repeat a few times, inviting her to join in. Raise your hand to your mouth as you create the sound to draw her attention to that part of your face.
● Make a different sound such as 'la, la, la.' Make a happy expression and invite her to copy you. Emphasise the use of your tongue in creating this sound.

● Use your mouth to create another sound such as, 'ah, ah, ah', keeping your mouth open as you pronounce each 'ah'.
● Each time, invite her to join in.
● If your baby makes a different sound, praise her efforts and copy her sound. Can she do it again?
● Now repeat the game, using some soft toys. Make up a different noise to represent the different toys. Let your baby hold the toys and encourage her to make up or copy a sound for each of them.

Taking it further
● Use a drum and as you beat it, say, 'Boom, boom, boom'. Repeat a few times.
● Use a small hand bell and tinkle it quietly. Alternate the quiet of the bell with the bang of a drum.

LEARNING OPPORTUNITIES
● To manipulate sound makers
● To encourage response to familiar songs and rhymes
● To develop an appreciation of music.

YOU WILL NEED
A medium-sized cushion; four different pieces of fabric (in contrasting colours to the cushion); four 'song buttons' (small microchips that play tunes when pressed, available from good craft shops); a needle and thread or sewing machine; glue.

Song cushion

Sharing the game
● Sit with your baby and allow him to watch as you create the exciting cushion for him.
● Make a cushion cover from the four pieces of brightly coloured fabric, by sewing the fabric to the cushion itself.
● Before you sew the fabric pieces to the cushion you need to fix the song buttons in place. You may do this by gluing them securely to the cushion. Place a song button under each different coloured piece of fabric. You may additionally secure them by stitching a patch around them, keeping them in a sort of pocket. This will also make it easier to identify where each one is.
● Once the cushion is completed, encourage your baby to touch and explore it. Can he find the tunes that are hidden under the fabric?
● Act surprised when he pushes and plays a tune each time.
● Repeat the tunes and encourage your baby to listen to them again. Sing along with the tunes, making up some actions for your baby to copy.
● Pretend that you can't make the song buttons work and invite your baby to help you. Praise him for finding the button and playing a tune. Repeat this game as many times as your baby wishes.

Taking it further
● Place some toys related to the tunes on the floor beside your baby. For example, as he hears the tune, 'Twinkle, Twinkle, Little Star', hold up a star and make it dance!

HEARING

LEARNING OPPORTUNITIES
● To manipulate objects to create sounds
● To aid muscular development
● To make sounds in response to songs.

YOU WILL NEED
Eight paper plates; scissors; coloured sheets of Cellophane; small bells; beads; buttons; glue; sticky tape.

Plate play

Sharing the game
● Take two of the plates, cutting a small shape out of the centre. Use sticky tape to attach a piece of coloured Cellophane over each hole.
● Now take three small bells and place them in between the two plates. Do this by placing the bells on one plate and then covering them up by sticking the other plate over the top with glue or sticky tape. Leave the plates to dry if you have used glue, so that they are securely joined.

● Repeat this process, varying the shapes that you cut out from the centre and the colours of Cellophane that you use.
● Inside each pair of plates place something like beads or buttons, that will make a sound when shaken. Always make sure that the plates are carefully fixed together so that the contents cannot escape!
● Finally fix a pair of plates together without adding anything between them. When shaken, you and your baby can enjoy the sound of silence.
● Let your baby experiment with the sounds she can make. Notice which sounds she seems to enjoy most. Act surprised when she manages to make a noise with the plates, to add to her enjoyment!

Taking it further
● When joining the plates, add in some lengths of ribbon so that they hang and move when your baby shakes them.
● Create some textured patterns on the outside of the plates.
● Allow your baby to decorate the outsides of the plates with finger paints.

HEARING

AGE RANGE
1-2 years

LEARNING OPPORTUNITIES
● To develop hand-to-eye co-ordination
● To encourage enjoyment of creation of sound
● To aid muscular development.

YOU WILL NEED
Lengths of strong string; a curtain pole; two sturdy chairs; strips of Cellophane and tin foil; bells; shoestrings; large bright beads; small kitchen utensils; baby rattles; spoons.

THINK FIRST!
Never leave your child unattended with lengths of string, shoestrings and so on.

Pole strips

Sharing the game
● Position two sturdy chairs a curtain pole length apart and rest the curtain pole between them, against the backs of the chairs. Secure them into place with some string. Check that your baby can sit next to or underneath the pole.
● Place the strips of Cellophane and foil, bells, large beads, rattles and shoestrings in a box on the floor.
● Let your baby explore the contents of the box while you create the 'sound pole' for him to explore.
● Sit next to your child. Thread a few beads onto one of the shoestrings or a short length of string and attach it to the pole so that it hangs down.
● Thread three or four bells onto another string. Again attach it to the pole.
● Next tie lengths of Cellophane, fabric and tin foil onto the pole.
● Lastly, attach a few of his old rattles to string and add them to the pole.
● Start by letting your child explore the hanging sound display and then offer him a spoon. Take one yourself and play some tunes together!

Taking it further
● Place the pole or line of sound makers higher so that your child can play when he is standing.
● Place the line in front of a mirror so that your child can watch himself at work.

HEARING

AGE RANGE
1-2 years

LEARNING OPPORTUNITIES
● To develop hand-to-eye co-ordination
● To create a sound maker
● To encourage stretching and pushing movements.

YOU WILL NEED
Empty stacking crisp cartons; wrapping paper; felt-tipped pens; coins; pegs; beads; stones; sticky tape (patterned or holographic if possible); white paper; glue.

Roll a shake

Sharing the game
● Gather all the items together and place them on the floor ensuring that any small or unsuitable items are out of reach of your child. Allow her to play with the crisp cartons and wrapping paper while you create the set of 'toys'.
● Take some sheets of white paper and use the felt-tipped pens to create bold shapes and patterns on the paper.

● Cover one or two of the empty stacking cartons with this decorated paper, attaching it with glue or sticky tape.
● Give your child a length of sticky tape to 'play with', ensuring that she does not try to eat it.
● Use some of the wrapping paper to 'jazz' up the other stacking cartons.
● Place some of the small items in each of the cartons, varying the quantities and types of object. Let your child help you, making sure that she does not place any small objects into her mouth, ears or nose!
● As she places the items inside the cartons, count aloud together. Invite her to add some more or say, 'I think that's plenty/enough'.
● Use the brightly coloured sticky tape to secure the lids.
● Sit opposite your child and roll the finished shakers to her. Encourage her to listen to the different sounds.
● Encourage her to roll the cartons back to you, pushing them out, stretching and reaching and pulling them back and letting them go.

Taking it further
● Try to build a tower with the 'sound cartons'. Hold them steady as your child adds each one.

HEARING

LEARNING OPPORTUNITIES
● To create sounds
● To listen to and recognise animal sounds
● To relate something visual to a sound.

YOU WILL NEED
Four empty crisp tubes; animal print paper or fabric (fake only) such as sheep, tiger, giraffe, frog and lion skin. Sound buttons (small microchips that make animal sounds when pressed), scissors and glue.

Animal sounds

Sharing the game
● Spend some time making animal sounds with your child. Make some sounds for him to guess and then ask him to make some animal sounds for you to recognise.
● Explain that you are going to make some animal sound shakers together. Decide which animals you will create by buying some 'sound buttons' and seeing which animal noises they make. If none are available, experiment with some sounds by shaking different objects inside your crisp tubes and seeing what animals they sound like. Ideas include dried pasta, coins, beads, buttons, marbles, pegs and pieces of silver foil.
● Once you have decided on your four animals, find four pieces of fabric or paper to represent them. Cut each piece to fit the length of the tube.
● Once you have covered the tubes and placed the sound makers (whether buttons or objects) inside, attach the lids securely.
● Place the four 'animals' on the floor and invite your child to explore them with you.

● Invite him to select one and listen to the noise it makes. Wait until he names it, or prompt him by saying, 'Oh, what was that?', or 'Did you hear that sound?'.
● If he doesn't suggest the animal's name or sound, you could name it for him. Talk about the animal print cover.
● Let your child roll the tubes around and play freely with them.

Taking it further
● Gather a selection of soft toy animals and encourage your child to make up some animal sounds, using everyday objects, to represent them.

HEARING

AGE RANGE
1-2 years

LEARNING OPPORTUNITIES
● To create similar sounds
● To explore sound making
● To manipulate and develop small muscles.

YOU WILL NEED
Eight empty sweet tubes; film canisters or something similar; pegs; coins; sugar; water; sticky tape.

Tube shakers

Sharing the game
● Choose two similar tubes and place a peg inside each one.
● In the next two tubes pour sugar until each one is half-full.
● Place four ten pence pieces in each of two further tubes.
● Pour a little amount of water into each of the final pair of containers.
● Use the sticky tape to securely close each tube, ensuring that your child cannot get hold of the contents of any of the tubes.
● Place them on the floor for your child to explore.
● Talk about the different sounds that your child has discovered. The pegs will make a slow sound as they move from one part of the tube to another, the coins will make a harsher sound than the soft scratchy sound of the sugar.

● Now encourage your child to find the matching pairs of tubes. Ask her, 'Does this one sound the same as this one?'.
● Continue exploring the sounds, suggesting which sound similar or different.

Taking it further
● Ask your child for some suggestions of other objects to place inside the tubes. Remind her that she needs to make a pair of matching sounds to play the game.
● Find some suitable items from your food cupboard for your child to shake under supervision (making sure that the lids are securely fastened). Ideas include sugar strands, gravy granules and dried fruit.

AGE RANGE
2-3 years

LEARNING OPPORTUNITIES
● To develop hand-to-eye co-ordination
● To listen to sounds created.

YOU WILL NEED
Plastic pipes, poster tubes or plastic two-litre bottles with the bottom cut off; ribbons; chains; scarves; beads; a basket.

Pipe music

Sharing the game
● Position a length of pipe (or alternative) at an angle, against a wall, chair back or low table. Make sure that your child will be able to post things down the pipe and be able to retrieve them.
● Place lengths of chain, scarves, strings of beads and ribbons into the basket on the floor near the pipe.
● Let your child explore the items in the basket.

● Sit with him and choose some chains from the basket. 'Pour' them into your palm, tapping them to create a sound.
● Take the ribbon and repeat the process, demonstrating how the ribbons don't make a sound when tapped.
● Next, choose a scarf and go to the length of pipe, roll the scarf into a loose ball and drop it through the pipe. Exclaim how it doesn't make much noise.
● Repeat the game with the string of beads. Does this make a noise? Let your child have as many turns as he wishes, exclaim at the sounds together.
● Now suggest that he tries with the chains.
● Repeat the game with each of the items in the basket.

Taking it further
● Talk and make sounds down the pipe. Your child will enjoy making funny noises and hearing the funny echoing sounds.

HEARING

LEARNING OPPORTUNITIES
● To appreciate that different materials have different sounds
● To use 'beaters' to create a range of sounds
● To encourage your child to help other people.

YOU WILL NEED
A long length of bright cord; a length of plastic tubing; a length of pipe; a metal kitchen utensil or piece of copper piping; a roll of cardboard; a wooden spoon and a metal spoon.

THINK FIRST!
Do not leave your child unattended with the lengths of cord and pipes.

Pan pipes

Sharing the game
● Gather all the pipes and tubes together. Suggest that your child chooses two to carry.
● Take the pipes into the garden. Ask her to hold one end of the cord as you unravel it.
● Attach your end to a bush, tree or washing pole. Walk back to your child and thank her for holding it. Ask her to help you to attach it to something secure.

● Invite her to pass the various types of pipe to you one at a time.
● Use strong tape to attach small pieces of cord onto each individual pipe. Securely tie each pole or tube to the length of cord by tying the small pieces of cord onto the long piece.
● Space out the pipes so that they hang freely, but if moved slightly will knock together.
● When the pipes are all in place offer your child a spoon, taking the other yourself. Begin to play the pipes together.
● Show your child how to tap each one gently, then a little harder.
● Run your spoon first one way and then the other along the arrangement of pipes. Help your child to do the same.

Taking it further
● Add bright ribbons to hang between the pipes and tubes.
● Hang the pipes and tubes against a fence or length of wood. They will sound different when tapped.

HEARING

AGE RANGE
2-3 years

LEARNING OPPORTUNITIES
● To develop listening and concentration skills
● To encourage recognition and response
● To stimulate and motivate.

YOU WILL NEED
A tape recorder; a tape; a camera (a Polaroid camera would be ideal – if not process the film to complete this activity).

Whose voice?

Sharing the game
● Sit with your child, explain what the tape recorder is for. Demonstrate what you mean by using it to record yourself saying, 'Hello Ben, how are you?'.
● Play the recording back to him a few times. Explain that you have recorded your voice. Offer to record his. Record his voice and play it back to him. Let him listen to the recordings several times.
● Continue to familiarise him with the idea of recording and playing back by singing a little of his favourite song then suggesting he sings a little too. Play it back and enjoy the song together.
● Now record various family members as they are visiting (with their permission). Each time encourage them to say something to your child.
● Take photographs of all the people that recorded messages for your child.
● When you have processed the photographs, you can play a matching game.
● Place out the photographs of the people. Let your child look at them, naming each one.

● Explain that you are going to let him hear their voices. Play the voices, one by one and suggest that he points to whoever he hears.
● Don't worry if he gets it wrong, give him some more time to listen and praise him, saying, 'Good try. Let's listen closely again.'. Play it again and have another try.

Taking it further
● Record some of your child's toys that speak or make a noise. Place them in a box and play the recording of the various sounds. Encourage him to match the sound to the toy.

AGE RANGE
2-3 years

LEARNING OPPORTUNITIES
● To investigate an area
● To develop attention span
● To encourage listening and responding.

YOU WILL NEED
A few toys that play a simple tune or make a sound; cushions; pieces of fabric; towels; a box.

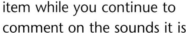

Sound hunt

Sharing the game
● Place three or four toys that make a sound into a box on the floor. Ideas include a clock, a music box, a toy that talks or laughs, a stopwatch or a toy engine.

● Lift each one in turn and draw your child's attention to the sounds it makes. Let your child explore the item while you continue to comment on the sounds it is making.

● Once all of the sounds and toys have been explored suggest that he turns away and hides his eyes while you hide the items under cushions, fabric and towels.

● If your child finds it easier, let her hide the toys for you to find, watching what you do, so that they understand how to play when it is their turn.

● Once the items are hidden, activate the noises one by one and invite your child to find them.

● Play the game again, this time asking her to guess which toy is making the noise.

● Finally, turn each sound off and hide them again. Encourage your child to find the items by touch this time.

Taking it further
● Use a large cushion cover or pillowcase to place the sound-makers in. Add a new instrument and toy. Sit beside her on the floor. Tell her that you are going to put your hand in and switch on the sound. Can she guess what you have found?

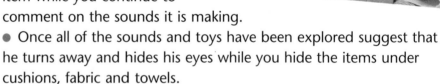

CHAPTER 7

Even the smallest baby responds to and also initiates interactions with people who give him sensitive attention. Communication between adults and babies and toddlers helps them to 'attune' their actions and expressions to each other. Interaction can extend any learning opportunity through the senses if used in an appropriate way.

SONG & RHYME TIME

BEGINNING TO TALK

Intuitively adults start singing action songs and nursery rhymes to babies, acknowledging that even though the baby cannot sing the words he can learn the actions and respond to the rhythm. The baby shows his enjoyment by eager attention and laughter.

The sequence of learning language usually follows a similar path for everyone. Most babies begin by using naming words – nouns. The more nouns (real objects/things) he explores through listening, touching, tasting and so on, the more vocabulary he will learn and grow in confidence to use.

How you can help
● Talk to your baby about everything. While you carry out routines, name the items you use. If out in the garden, name the things your child sees and touches.
● Play games to name parts of the body.
● Gather small sets of toys or household items for him to explore and as he selects them, name them.
● Look at books that have simple pictures, naming the items on the page, while pointing to them.
● Sing short rhymes and repeat them often. Where possible, relate the words in the rhymes to real items, naming them in the rhyme while offering them to your baby to explore.

READY FOR ACTION

As your child's vocabulary grows he will also start to use some describing words (adjectives) – obvious ones are 'hot' and 'sharp' which are essential concepts with respect to your child's safety. He will also begin to use a range of doing words (verbs). To help this vocabulary acquisition you can talk about the things that you are doing as you share time together. Describe what 'action' is happening while it is taking place. For example, say, 'Let's walk here!' (instead of just walking); or while he is eating lunch say, 'Oh, you're eating your soup' (rather than focusing on his ability to finish his portion).

How you can help
● Sing action songs with her, such as 'Put your finger on your nose' or 'Stand up, sit down, keep moving'. A good

source of action rhymes is the book, *Okki Tokki Unga* (A&C Black).

● Describe your child's actions as he does something. Repeat the words if he repeats the action to reinforce the vocabulary.

● Speak clearly and correctly so that your child hears exactly what you are saying.

USING LANGUAGE

The first step in using language is hearing it. Conversations about anything will encourage your baby to listen and hear. He will eventually participate with 'babbling'. It is important that you respond to his 'babbles'. Reply using 'real' words, so that he hears new words and increases his vocabulary.

How you can help

● Talk to him about anything and everything. Change the tone of your voice according to what you are saying.

● Use your facial expressions to animate your conversations. Visually and verbally respond to his 'chatter'.

● Use puppets and dolls to stimulate conversation.

● Use rhymes and songs to give 'shape' to your talk. This will help him to develop his sense of rhythm.

SINGING TOGETHER

Singing a wide range of songs together helps to build your young child's vocabulary. Using rhymes and songs makes language learning enjoyable. Sing short songs, repetitive songs, funny songs and slow songs.

How you can help

● Provide a range of toys and items that are linked to the rhymes and songs that you are sharing.

● While singing, encourage him to use other senses to experience the words he is hearing, such as touching head, shoulders, knees and toes.

● Repeat one or two verses of a song rather than singing all of the verses. Your child will soon try to join in.

● Surround your young child with a wide variety of music to listen to. Play different types of music, such as country, jazz, rock, pop and classical. Do not just use them as background music but concentrate and listen to them as well.

● Offer a wide variety of sound makers that your child can use to add extra sparkle to the songs and rhymes you share!

CLOSE UP

When talking and singing with your young child, put lots of expression in your voice and on your face. Get close to him as you talk so that he can watch your lips. Respond with excitement, leaning closer and softly touching him – this may encourage him to talk more.

How you can help

● Play games like 'peek-a-boo' and 'pat-a-cake', tapping him gently like patting a cake.

● Play finger and toe games such as 'Round and round the garden' or 'This little piggy' (both found in *This Little Puffin*, edited by Elizabeth Matterson (Puffin)). This is great fun, but also introduces vocabulary.

● Sitting close, singing quietly, and gently repeating tunes will develop a sense of comfort and security.

RHYME TIME

There are a huge number of traditional and modern rhymes to share and enjoy with your child. Introduce one and repeat it each day. Your child will enjoy the fact that he recognises the rhythm as well as the words. Each time you introduce a new rhyme, try to bring it to life so that your child can see and feel it, as well as hear it. If you can also stimulate the sense of taste or smell too, that would be a bonus!

How you can help

● Use real objects such as toys, utensils and natural items to bring the rhymes to life.

● Cut out pictures from colouring-in books to 'illustrate' the words.

● Use movement and music to bring appropriate rhymes to life.

● Enjoy sharing rhymes and songs as often as possible – at least every day. They are an ideal way to stimulate the use of language and to encourage your young child's development in a wide variety of ways.

LEARNING OPPORTUNITIES
● To develop an awareness of texture
● To develop hand-to-eye co-ordination
● To listen and respond to song.

YOU WILL NEED
A soft toy cat and dog; a cardboard illustration of a fiddle; a plastic cow; a moon shape cushion; a plastic bowl; small wooden spoon; a large box.

Hey Diddle, Diddle

Sharing the game
● Place all of the small items into the large box.
● Place the box on the floor beside some cushions.
● Sit with your baby beside the box.
● Slowly lift the lid so that the items can be seen.
● Explore the items, encouraging your baby to copy you and join in.
● As you lift out an item, describe it and then offer it to him.
● Say the rhyme, 'Hey Diddle, Diddle' (traditional) and show your baby the various items as you say each line from the poem.
● Bring the rhyme to life by extending your mimes, using the objects. For example, pretend to use the dish and spoon to eat; pretend the cat is playing the fiddle; let the cow jump over the moon and make the dog laugh.
● Sing snippets of the rhyme as your baby touches and manipulates the various visual aids in the box.

Taking it further
● As you say each of the lines, place the item related to it in front of your baby, but out of reach. Repeat the song, pointing to the 'visual aid' to encourage your baby to reach for it.

LEARNING OPPORTUNITIES
● To introduce a variety of scents
● To explore a range of textures
● To listen to poems and rhymes.

YOU WILL NEED
Three types of real flowers; a range of plastic and silk flowers; silver bells; large shells; cardboard (stiff); glue; scissors; material swatches; felt-tipped pens; a large basket; lavender; pot pourri; needle and thread; the rhyme 'Mary, Mary Quite Contrary' (Traditional).

Mary, Mary

Sharing the game

● Draw some flower shapes onto a large sheet of cardboard. Use glue to stick a few shells onto the drawings to make flower-heads. Draw the stems and leaves in proportion.

● Before gluing the shells down, place a small amount of lavender or pot pourri under the shells.

● Place the real flowers, plastic flowers and silk flowers into the basket.

● Sew some bells onto a few of the silk flower heads.

● Sit with your baby and encourage her to explore the flowers in the basket. Look at the cardboard shell flowers together.

● Lift some to your nose, exclaiming at the scents.

● Draw your child's attention to the noise of the 'bell' flowers and the feel of the 'shell' flowers.

● Now say the traditional rhyme, 'Mary, Mary Quite Contrary', pausing to smell, shake or touch the flowers, encouraging your baby to join in. Repeat the rhyme several times, each time lifting a different flower for her to explore.

Taking it further

● Walk around the house singing the rhyme, while pointing to pictures, fabrics or photographs of flowers.

● Sing the rhyme while arranging flowers in a vase.

● In the garden, explore the grass, flowers and trees together.

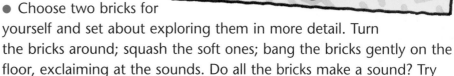

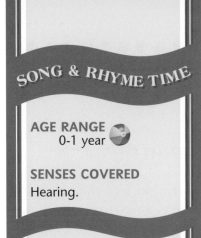

SONG & RHYME TIME

AGE RANGE
0-1 year

SENSES COVERED
Hearing.

LEARNING OPPORTUNITIES
● To develop an appreciation of sound
● To encourage sound making
● To develop the sense of touch.

YOU WILL NEED
Wooden bricks; plastic bricks; material bricks; small cardboard boxes; a large metal box (turned over to become a large brick!); a Humpty Dumpty toy (or soft toy to play the part); the rhyme, 'Humpty Dumpty' (page 127).

Humpty Dumpty

Sharing the game

● Place all the bricks inside the large metal box. Place the box on the floor.
● Sit with your baby on the floor and open the box.
● Take out two bricks yourself and encourage your baby to copy you and explore the contents of the box.
● If your baby doesn't take any bricks out of the box, take some more out and offer him yours to explore.
● Choose two bricks for yourself and set about exploring them in more detail. Turn the bricks around; squash the soft ones; bang the bricks gently on the floor, exclaiming at the sounds. Do all the bricks make a sound? Try out the different types and talk about what you are doing.
● Make sure that your baby is watching what you are doing, so that he can copy some of your ideas with his own chosen bricks. Help him to experiment with his own ideas.
● Next, pile the bricks one on top of another. Let your baby hand them to you so that he is helping.
● Build a wall so that he can knock it down.
● As you are exploring and experimenting, sing the 'Humpty Dumpty' rhyme on page 127.
● Sit your Humpty Dumpty toy on the top of the wall as you say the rhyme, toppling him off at the appropriate moment!

Taking it further

● Pretend to be a horse and 'help' Humpty. Gather a few toy horses and a doll to be the helpers.

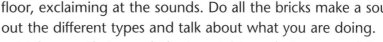

AGE RANGE
0-1 year

SENSES COVERED
Taste.

LEARNING
OPPORTUNITIES
● To develop pincer grip and grasp
● To develop hand-to-eye co-ordination
● To stimulate the sense of taste.

YOU WILL NEED
Finger puppets; a range of cereals; soft crisps; fruit pieces; small bowls; the rhyme, 'Tommy Thumb' (Traditional).

Tommy Thumb

Sharing the game
● Gather a selection of finger puppets. These are available from catalogues and high street stores.
● Put a little of each type of cereal, fruit and crisps into the bowls.
● Place a puppet on one of your thumbs. Sit opposite your baby and tell her that your Tommy Thumb puppet is going to choose some things to eat!
● Use the puppet (on your thumb) and your index finger to choose something to eat from the bowls. Say, 'This is Tommy Thumb and he likes strawberries.'.
● Offer the strawberry to your baby, saying, 'Tommy Thumb wants you to have this strawberry.'.
● Repeat the game, choosing a different sort of food.
● Invite your baby to try the puppet on her thumb. Can she use it to select a piece of food?
● Next, sing the rhyme 'Tommy Thumb' (Traditional) to your baby, making the puppet move to the words, as directed in the actions.

● At the end of the song enjoy the rest of the snacks, moving Tommy Thumb in a dancing fashion to retrieve them!

Taking it further
● Sit opposite your baby and use your hands and arms to tell the rhyme, 'Tommy Thumb'.
● Draw little faces or animals onto strips of paper. Use sticky tape to attach one to each of your fingertips. Tell your baby some more rhymes with people or animals in them, such as 'Two little dicky birds' or 'Five little ducks' (both found in *This Little Puffin*, edited by Elizabeth Matterson (Puffin)).

SENSES COVERED
Taste.

LEARNING OPPORTUNITIES
● To listen and respond to rhymes
● To identify fruits by name
● To develop physical skills.

YOU WILL NEED
Apples; grapes; strawberries; bananas; bowls; a small, clean bucket; a male doll; a female doll.

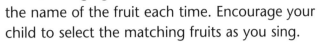

THINK FIRST!
Make sure the box will bear his weight and hold his hand at all times.

Jack and Jill

Sharing the game

● Sit with your child and sing the traditional rhyme, 'Jack and Jill'.
● Sing it a second time and hold up the two dolls and the bucket at the appropriate parts of the song.
● Sing the song a third time, introducing a new line, such as: 'Jack and Jill went up the hill to fetch a pail of apples'!
● As you sing the word 'apples', ask your child to help you to gather the apples, putting them in the bucket. (Make sure that your child understands that the word 'pail' is another word for bucket.)
● Once you have gathered all the fruits, prepare them to eat. Let your child help by handing the fruits to you to rinse and cut.

● Place the cut fruits into two bowls – one for you and one for your child.
● Sing the song several more times, changing the name of the fruit each time. Encourage your child to select the matching fruits as you sing.
● Help your child to use the dolls to pretend they are lifting the fruits to put into the bucket!

Taking it further

● Focus on the 'up the hill' part of the rhyme. Place a few cushions for your child to climb 'up' and over. Place a strong box upside-down and help him to climb it.

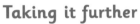

LEARNING OPPORTUNITIES
● To explore a range of materials
● To experiment with a variety of textures
● To respond to songs and rhymes.

YOU WILL NEED
Flour; water; dough; bowls; spoons; cake tin; the rhyme, 'Pat-a-cake, Pat-a-cake' on page 127.

Pat-a-cake

Sharing the game

● Share the traditional rhyme, 'Pat-a-cake'. Perform simple clapping actions with your child.

● Now take three bowls and place different stages of play dough in each.

● In the first bowl, place the ready to use home-made dough (see the recipe on page 125).

● In the second bowl, place a dough that is a little too runny and soft.

● In the third bowl, place some flour and water ready to mix.

● Place all the bowls on a low table and let your child explore each bowl while you sing the rhyme again.

● Use a spoon to stir the mixture and give your child a spoon. Let her join in. Try to remain relaxed about the mess!

● When your child has had plenty of time to experiment with and stir the gooey mixtures, encourage her to concentrate on manipulating the ready-made dough.

● Suggest that your child places the ready-made dough in the cake tin. Help her to manipulate it up to the edges of the tin by pressing and patting.

● Sing the song again as, together, you attempt to make the runny mixtures into proper usable play dough!

Taking it further

● Place a ready-made cake on a plate. Make some icing and then invite your child to spoon it and spread it on the cake.

● Allow your child to help cut a real cake.

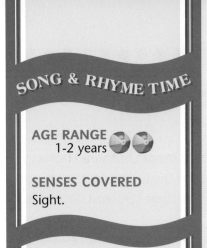
SENSES COVERED
Sight.

LEARNING OPPORTUNITIES
● To visually stimulate
● To develop hand-to-eye co-ordination
● To listen and respond to rhymes.

YOU WILL NEED
Black felt; cardboard; holographic paper; Velcro; scissors; glue; bowl; cushion; the rhyme, 'Twinkle, Twinkle, Little Star' (Traditional).

Twinkle, twinkle

Sharing the game
● Cover a cushion or large piece of stiff cardboard with a piece of black felt.
● Take another piece of card and cover it in the holographic paper. Glue it in place.
● Cut out star shapes from the holographic covered card.
● Attach a piece of Velcro (the side with the 'hoops') onto each star.
● Place the stars into the bowl. Place the bowl onto the floor and place the black cushion or board nearby.
● Sing the traditional song, 'Twinkle, Twinkle, Little Star' and encourage your child to choose a star and hang it on the board or cushion.

● Repeat a few times until all the stars are hung.
● Sing the song again, this time taking the stars from the 'sky' and placing them back into the bowl.
● Now move to an empty space with your child and sit down with the bowl beside you. Sing the song again and invite your child to take out the stars and place them in between you, in a circle.

Taking it further
● Use some of the stars to hold up above your head while saying the rhyme.
● Attach a star to a stick covered in silver foil. Twirl the stick above your head as you sing the rhyme.

SENSES COVERED
Smell

LEARNING OPPORTUNITIES
● To stimulate the sense of smell
● To develop vocabulary
● To relate words to pictures.

YOU WILL NEED
White card; felt-tipped pens; a small bowl; small wicker basket; small flower pot; glitter; peppermint tea leaves; herbs; pot pourri; perfume; cotton wool balls; glue; flower petals; photographs of the people taking part in this activity; the rhyme, 'Twinkling stars' on page 127.

Twinkling stars

Sharing the game
● Cut out some small cards from the white card. On the first one, draw some stars, on the second, draw some birds and on the third, draw a few flowers. Make a duplicate set, so that you and your child can play the game together.
● Glue a little glitter and some peppermint tea leaves onto the star cards.

● Glue some herbs and pot pourri onto the bird cards.
● Glue some petals onto the flower cards.
● Make some more white cards and glue photographs of anyone who is joining in. Spray a little perfume onto each photo card.
● Place the star cards in the small bowl, the bird cards in the wicker basket and the flower cards in the flower pot. Put the photo cards beside them.
● Sing verse one of the song, 'Twinkling stars' on page 127 and choose a star card, encouraging your child to copy you and do the same.
● Sing verse two, picking up the bird cards; verse three, picking up the flowers and verse four, choosing photographs of the various people with you today. Encourage your child to continue to copy you.

Taking it further
● Sit on the floor with your child. Sing the song, and at each verse, place all the cards around you both creating a circle.
● Repeat the song, pointing to the cards that relate to the words.

SENSES COVERED
Touch.

LEARNING OPPORTUNITIES
● To listen and respond to rhymes
● To explore a variety of textures
● To develop fine motor skills.

YOU WILL NEED
A toy black sheep; a male doll (the master); a female doll (the dame); another doll (the little boy); cotton wool balls; two balls of wool; some sheep fleece (you can find this snagged on hedgerows and in fields where sheep have been grazing – remember to wash it first); pillow case; three small boxes.

THINK FIRST!
Make sure that your child washes his hands after handling the fleece.

Baa, Baa, Black Sheep

Sharing the game
● In one box place the cotton wool balls, in the second box place the balls of wool and in the third box place the real wool.
● Gather the sheep and dolls and place them along with the boxes into the pillow case.
● Sit with your child and begin singing the rhyme, 'Baa, Baa, Black Sheep'. Invite him to take out the black sheep from the pillow case and play with it.
● Take out the boxes and explore them together.
● Sing the rhyme again and take out the 'master', 'dame' and 'little boy' and 'give' them some wool each.
● Draw your child's attention to the textures, length, colour and smell of the different types of wool.
● Now let him have some time to freely explore the items and ask him to sort the various wools back into the boxes.
● Unravel some of the balls of wool. Cut a short piece from each type of wool. Lie them beside each other to compare.
● Talk about which type of wool is the shortest, longest, softest, fluffiest and so on.

Taking it further
● Look at some pictures and story books that have pictures or photographs of sheep in them.
● Talk about what sheep eat and where they live.
● Look around for things made of wool to show to your child.

AGE RANGE
2-3 years

SENSES COVERED
Sight.

LEARNING OPPORTUNITIES
● To relate visual clues to songs
● To respond to visual stimuli
● To develop vocabulary.

YOU WILL NEED
A range of visual aids; a wooden star; a plastic duck; a mechanical horse; a soft doll; a plastic dish and spoon; a large box.

Song time

Sharing the game
● Place all the toys in a box and sit near to the box with your child.
● Suggest you sing some songs together. What are her favourite ones? If she does not choose any songs that relate to the objects in the box, then gently suggest one or two to get the game started!
● Sing a few songs together and then pretend that you have just remembered that there are some things in the box that remind you of the songs!
● Take the box and suggest that she looks inside it.
● Let her explore the contents of the box. Do any of the items remind her of the songs she has just been singing? Which ones and why?
● Suggest that she selects a toy. Respond by singing a related song – or wait for her to suggest what you should sing.
● Now sing a line from a song and invite her to identify which visual goes with it.
● Talk about each visual as she selects it – describe it and pretend to play with it.

Taking it further
● Add new visuals to your box to relate to the various songs and rhymes she knows.
● Hide the visuals from the box around the room and ask her to help you find a specific item while you sing the matching song.
● Place the visuals around her room and select a few songs to sing before she goes to sleep.

AGE RANGE
2-3 years

SENSES COVERED
Hearing.

LEARNING OPPORTUNITIES
● To develop vocabulary
● To develop listening and concentration skills
● To encourage your child to explore a range of objects.

YOU WILL NEED
A small bell; a shaker; a rattle; a squeaky toy; a watch; a small music box; a doll or teddy with sounds; a few small material pouches or bags; ribbon.

Lucy Locket

Sharing the game
● Gather the various sound makers and place some around the area where you normally play with your child. Hide a few too.
● Offer him a 'pocket' or small bag and take one yourself. Place a ribbon round each one.
● Say the traditional rhyme, 'Lucy Locket' (found in good nursery rhyme compilations). Pretend together that you both have the 'pocket' that Lucy Locket lost.
● Suggest that you find things to put into the pockets.
● Look and find a few of the hidden or placed items. Name them as you find them.
● Sit together and explore the various items commenting on the sounds each one makes.
● Name each of the items again as you explore them and describe the sounds they make.
● Play a game of hiding the sound makers behind your back, shaking or playing them and then asking your child to guess which one you are hiding.

Taking it further
● Suggest that your child takes his 'pocket' of items and hides them for you to find. Say the rhyme together as you look.
● Go into other rooms and gather items to place in the 'pockets', then explore them together.

AGE RANGE
2-3 years

SENSES COVERED
Sight.

LEARNING
OPPORTUNITIES
● To develop hand-to-eye
co-ordination
● To develop an
awareness of texture
● To develop visual
awareness.

YOU WILL NEED
A large black pom-pom
and a pair of black rolled-
up socks, or a hand
puppet of a spider. A few
trays; silver foil; cotton
wool; bells; foil cartons;
empty plastic bottles;
sticky tape; the rhyme,
'Incy Wincy Spider' on
page 128.

Incy Wincy Spider

Sharing the game

● Place the trays on the floor. Place a different material in each tray –
silver foil, cotton wool and so on.

● Say the 'Incy Wincy Spider' rhyme using your (improvised or ready-
made) spider puppet to act it out as you say it.

● Hold the puppet near to the variously-filled trays.

● Now say the rhyme again, this time dropping the spider into one of
the trays, as you say the line, 'wash the spider out'.

● Draw your child's attention to the noise that the 'spider' makes
when it drops into the various trays.

● Next, take an empty two litre bottle and cut off each end. Use
sticky tape to cover any sharp edges.

● Explain that this can be the 'water spout' in the rhyme and show
your child how to drop the spider puppet down the pipe at the
appropriate point in the rhyme!

● Repeat this a few times encouraging her to drop the spider. Make it
into a game, trying to catch the spider after she has dropped it down
the pipe! Let her have a turn to try and catch the spider too.

Taking it further

● Hold the 'pipe' over the trays and drop the spider through.
Encourage your child to anticipate and catch the spider.

CHAPTER 8

STORY TIME

It is never too early to 'read' books to your baby. Books and stories should be a part of your everyday routine. Using bright, interesting books to look at and talk about gives your baby the idea that books are fun.

SHARING BOOKS

Sharing books and stories with your baby or young child is one of the most intimate, secure and pleasurable experiences that you can have together. Reading the same stories over and again gives your toddler a wonderful sense of security and he will love to join in with favourite phrases. He will probably want to point out the same, as well as new things that he spots in the illustrations and it is important that you maintain the high level of enthusiasm that you mustered for the first reading. We must remember, as storytellers, to recognise the need to use the correct wording time after time. This increases your young child's sense of security and they will enjoy the familiarity of the pictures, words and props.

As well as reading old favourites, it is important to continue to introduce new and exciting stories as well. This will encourage your child to explore new ideas and scenarios, as well as being comforted by those he recognises.

How you can help

● From the earliest years, your baby will learn that looking at books is enjoyable and special. Hearing favourite stories over and over will help to develop his thinking and understanding.
● Allow your baby to do the work! As he looks at the pictures on the pages and hears the words you are reading, his brain will be hard at work.
● Using all of his senses to extend the experience of books is an ideal way to help your young child gain more from storytelling.

THE READING ROUTINE

Just as we make time for feeding, sleeping, shopping and cleaning, it is vital that we make regular times to share books. Choose a time each day to snuggle up comfortably with a good selection of books. Make it special and exciting by gathering drinks, any props and a cosy quilt and blanket.

As well as a regular routine reading session, hold some more spontaneous reading sessions, perhaps while you are eating a snack or at times of the day when your child needs to rest or calm down!

On a cold day jump into your child's bed together, turn on a lamp and snuggle up with some favourite stories.

Let your child see you read as well. Talk about what you are reading, whether it is a medical encyclopaedia, a magazine or a favourite novel!

How you can help
● Give him a variety of books – cloth, vinyl, board and textured.
● Hold him close, cuddling him gently as you read or talk about the pictures in a book.
● Make story time a special part of your everyday activities.
● Choose books that will interest him. If he likes cars or animals choose books with these items or characters in. Allow him to choose books from a selection of appropriate ones.
● Visit a library together, on a regular basis. Show him how to care for books and treat them as precious objects.
● Let your child turn the pages when you indicate that it is time.
● Change your voice to imitate the characters during stories. This

may take some practice before you can do this effectively. If you find this difficult then remember to include lots of expression in your voice. Your child will be gripped by a story if you make it sound exciting, sad, scary or fun!

TALKING ABOUT STORIES
Using books is not just about 'reading'. There is a great deal of value in discussing and describing the pictures and relating them to your child's 'real' world. Children will often voice any fears and anxieties when prompted by a story, as they will often recognise a character or situation that they have been trying to deal with recently themselves. Two- to three-year-olds benefit hugely from this sort of discussion. Many children of this age will have developed enough vocabulary to begin talking about what they see and what is happening in the books. If they are very familiar with the book they may also be able to predict what is about to happen from memory or become involved in recalling the story.

How you can help
● Go through books slowly, calling attention to the pictures, the sounds and any textures.
● Explore the content of the book. Extend the words by relating the story to your child's experiences.
● Follow up your stories with real life experiences. For example, if you are reading a book about the farm, then show your child some pictures and photographs of farms, or go for a drive in the countryside to look at some. If you are reading about a garden, take him into the garden and talk about the things that he recognises from the story.

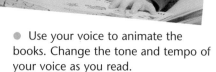

● Use your voice to animate the books. Change the tone and tempo of your voice as you read.
● Remember that often the best choice is to 'read' the same book again.

READING TOGETHER
Babies and young children have to be able to hear you clearly. When listening to stories and looking at books, they need to be able to distinguish sounds and words, so they can understand and follow what is being said.

Cut out as much background noise as possible – turn off the television and radio. Sit somewhere comfortable where you can both easily look at and see the whole book. It may be that if the book is large, the best place is lying on the floor.

How you can help
● Put time aside to enjoy books and stories together.
● Have a place to go when there are no distractions, and your child is eager to listen.
● Use books to stimulate all of his senses not just to 'read'.

AGE RANGE
0-1 year

LEARNING OPPORTUNITIES
● To develop an awareness of textures
● To develop manipulation skills
● To become familiar with bath books.

YOU WILL NEED
A bath book (plastic covered story book) such as *Elmer's Bath* by David McKee (Red Fox); items which relate to the story content (in this case, a duck, a ball, a bird); sponges; a bath; a bowl; a towel.

Bath books

Sharing the game

● Sit with your baby on her towel and together look at the bath book. Talk about the items in the pictures.
● Cut out, from a sponge, the shape of one of the items in the book, such as a bird or a fish.
● Let your baby play with the sponge shape.
● Dribble some water onto the shape. Show your baby what you are doing.
● Encourage your baby to lift the water-laden sponge shape. Help her to hold it over the bath or a bowl. Encourage her to squeeze it and feel the water trickle out.

● Give her the other items to play with while you fill the bath.
● When the bath is ready, suggest that she drops a ball or a duck into it (or whatever other toys you have chosen to go with the bath book).
● Place her in the bath and give her the bath book again. Look at the pictures together and then show her the matching items in the bath. Allow her some free time to explore the book and the objects.

Taking it further

● Use a face cloth to hide the items in the bath. Place your finger over the picture in the book and play hide and find.
● Dry the bath items off and allow your child to continue exploring them after bath time, perhaps while you are drying her and getting her ready for bed.

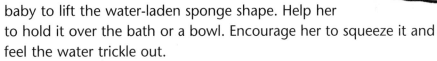

AGE RANGE
0-1 year

LEARNING OPPORTUNITIES
● To explore a variety of textures
● To listen to and look at a variety of visuals and words
● To develop focus of attention.

YOU WILL NEED
A cloth book which is bright and offers a variety of textured pictures, such as *Snail* by Fiona Watt (Usborne); a real item which reflects one of the objects in the book (such as a flower), or a toy relating to the book (such as a butterfly puppet); a basket.

Cloth books

Sharing the game
● Sit with your baby and look at the book together.
● Use the cloth book, encouraging him to follow a 'trail' through the book by drawing your finger along the pages to find a textured picture.
● Exclaim as you find a texture and describe what you feel.
● Encourage him to do this too. As he touches a picture, name what it is, such as a 'flower', 'leaf' or 'plant pot'.

● Look through the book a few times. Each time, encourage him to explore the pictures.
● Now show your baby the items relating to the book. Explore them together.
● Choose one of the items and show your baby how you look for the matching object in the book.
● Repeat this game, reversing the process – looking at the pictures in the book first then 'matching' them with the real items.

Taking it further
● Make a cloth book for your baby.
● Use small pieces of material or a few flannels. Choose material with a few simple pictures or patterns on it and glue scraps of these fabrics to the material 'pages'.
● Sew all the 'pages' together, along one edge, to create the book.

STORY TIME

AGE RANGE
0-1 year

LEARNING OPPORTUNITIES
● To encourage emotional response to books
● To use pictures to stimulate sight
● To develop a sense of curiosity.

YOU WILL NEED
A large lift-the-flap book with simple colourful illustrations (such as *Night, Night Baby* by Marie Birkinshaw (Ladybird)); a range of toys relating to the pictures in the book; small boxes or pieces of fabric.

Oh, it's a...

Sharing the game
● Sit with your baby on the floor – place her between your legs (so she is facing away from you), so that you can support her as she sits.
● Turn each page of the book, saying the rhyme or reading the simple story. On each page, lift the flap and respond to what is underneath.
● As you lift each flap exclaim, 'Oh, it's a...!'.
● Place your toys that relate to the story (such as a panda, rabbit and lion) in separate boxes or under pieces of fabric.
● This time, as you read the book again, lift-the-flap and then make a big show of either lifting the lid of the box or the piece of material.
● Let her pick up each toy to explore before moving on to the next page and box.
● Talk about each item – their colour, size, and the sounds they make.

Taking it further
● Place a few lift-the-flap books into a basket and share them, delighting in the surprises underneath each of the flaps.
● Make your own lift-the-flap book. Cut out pictures from wrapping paper and stick each picture on to an individual page. Place a flap over the top of each one. Enjoy it with your child.

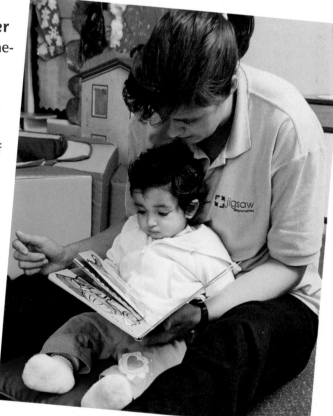

STORY TIME

LEARNING OPPORTUNITIES

● To develop awareness of sounds
● To explore a range of farm animals
● To stimulate interest in books.

YOU WILL NEED

A picture book about farm animals, ideas include *Farm Babies* and *Noisy Farm* both by Rod Campbell (Puffin) and *Fergus's Big Splash* by Tony Maddox (Piccadilly Press); some toy animals; a mirror; white card; black felt-tipped pens.

Farm time

Sharing the game

● Sit with your baby on your knee, look in the mirror and encourage your baby to do the same. Point at your baby then at yourself in the mirror.
● Look at the next pages in the book and point out one of the animals or a farm machine. Make an appropriate sound to go with the picture and point to it as you do so.
● Continue the game, pointing to different things in the book, making the appropriate sounds as you go.
● In between each animal or farm picture look into the mirror and say hello to yourself and your baby!
● Draw some patterns onto the pieces of card – squiggles, zig-zags, curves, squares and so on. Look at these together, alternating between looking at farm pictures and looking at pattern cards. Talk about the patterns together and trace along them with your baby's finger.

Taking it further

● Look at other books and pictures that include animals.
● Go for a drive or a walk in the countryside, if possible. Draw your baby's attention to the farms, tractors and animals that you come across. If you do not live in the countryside try finding out about the excellent city farms that are attached to many cities.

LEARNING OPPORTUNITIES
● To develop an awareness of the garden
● To stimulate the sense of smell
● To develop motor skills.

YOU WILL NEED
A book relating to flowers and gardens (such as *Humphrey's Garden* by Sally Hunter (Puffin)); a selection of real flowers of different kinds and colours; a basket.

THINK FIRST!
Remember to tell your child that they must not pick flowers unless you say it is alright to do so, as some might be poisonous or harmful.

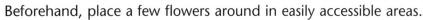

In the garden

Sharing the game
● Read the story, drawing the child's attention to the pictures. Name the colours, the characters and the types of flowers.
● If using the suggested book, *Humphrey's Garden*, draw attention to the flowers for Humphrey's mum and pretend to smell them. If using another book, then pretend to smell some of the flowers in the book.
● Move into the garden or to a park area.
Beforehand, place a few flowers around in easily accessible areas.
● Hold your child's hand and help her to carry the basket. Collect the flowers. Each time she picks one up, name it and mention what colour it is.
● Once you have gathered a variety in the basket, sit together and enjoy the scents.
● Read the book again, calling attention to the colours and smells of the flowers.

Taking it further
● Cut some circles from sheets of white paper.
● Offer your child some crayons or chubby pencils that are the same colours as the fresh flowers you have picked up.
● Use the crayons to create flower pictures.

STORY TIME

LEARNING OPPORTUNITIES
● To encourage response through sounds
● To encourage interaction
● To bring a story to life.

YOU WILL NEED
A book about the farm, such as *Can You Moo Too?* By David Wojtowycz (Orchard Books); a range of farm animals – wooden, plastic and soft; three boxes.

Animal sounds?

Sharing the game
● Gather all the farm toys. If possible, find ones that reflect the animals in the book you have chosen.
● Place the animals into the boxes – soft animals in one box, plastic animals in a second box and wooden animals in a third.
● While you turn the pages, 'read' the sounds that the animals make. Encourage your child to respond by copying the sound you make. Repeat the sounds a few times. Praise all his attempts at copying the sounds.
● Read the story again and as you come to an animal in the book, invite your child to choose a toy that matches with the illustrations.
● Next, hold up a toy and challenge your child to name it and then to find it in the book.

● Finally, try making an animal sound and suggest that he finds the illustration or toy that goes with the sound.

Taking it further
● On a piece of paper draw a cow's face bit by bit. Challenge your child to guess what animal it will be. Give your child some clues by making the animal's sound.
● Repeat this game with different animals, such as a pig, a horse and a duck.

LEARNING OPPORTUNITIES
● To listen and respond to instructions
● To develop an awareness of the environment
● To recognise familiar items.

YOU WILL NEED
A baby bath; a book about bath time, such as *Bathtime* (Dorling Kindersley); a bath duck; two small boats; three plastic or sponge fish; bath mitt; soap; sponge; towel; a large bowl.

Fun in the bath

Sharing the game
● Sit with your child beside the bath. Ask her to take her clothes off. As she attempts to remove an item, ask, 'What are you taking off?'. Provide as much help as is required. Fold the items and make a washing pile.

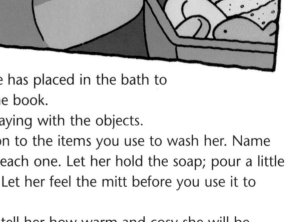

● Invite her to say which piece of clothing she will take off next.
● Continue until she is in her nappy or pants.
● Suggest she sits down and helps you to choose items to place in the bath from the bowl of objects listed in the panel.
● Encourage her to name each thing as she selects it and puts it in the bath.
● Look at the book together, encouraging her to relate the items she has placed in the bath to those in the pictures of the book.
● Enjoy the bath time, playing with the objects.
● Next, draw her attention to the items you use to wash her. Name them and let her explore each one. Let her hold the soap; pour a little shampoo into her hands. Let her feel the mitt before you use it to wash her.
● Hold up the towel and tell her how warm and cosy she will be when you wrap her in it. Smell it and exclaim, 'Oh, lovely!', rub it on your cheek saying 'Oh, how soft!'.
● Lift her out and enjoy drying time.

Taking it further
● Let her use all the items to bath her doll or teddy in a plastic bowl.

AGE RANGE
1-2 years

LEARNING OPPORTUNITIES
● To highlight the importance of routines
● To explore a variety of textures
● To enjoy sharing books.

YOU WILL NEED
A book illustrating getting ready for bed, such as *Night, Night, Cuddly Bear* by Martin Waddell, illustrated by Penny Dale (Walker Books) or *Mog and me* by Judith Kerr (HarperCollins); pyjamas; toothbrush; towel; toothpaste; dressing gown; flannel.

Goodnight, sleep tight

Sharing the game
● Look at your chosen book together. Read it through, drawing your child's attention to the various items relating to bedtime that are illustrated in the book.
● Wrap all of the items you have gathered inside the towel ready for your child to find.
● Give him the towel to look at and as he finds each

object, encourage him to name it, by asking, 'What have you found?'. Alternatively describe it for him.
● Ask lots of questions such as, 'Where are your pyjamas?'; 'Where is your teddy?'.
● As you look through the book again talk about the routine that the characters in the story are following. Is it the same as your child's bedtime routine?

● Suggest that he matches any real items with the items illustrated in the book if possible.

Taking it further
● Use the book as a list of things to gather before bedtime. Help your child to 'read' the book and point out or place the items onto a towel.
● Suggest 'It's time to brush your teeth!' or 'It's time to wash your face!'. Encourage him to select the items needed to carry out these routines.

LEARNING OPPORTUNITIES

● To listen and respond to stories
● To relate real items to pictures
● To listen to and identify sounds.

YOU WILL NEED

A book involving a baby interacting with a range of items, such as *Baby Knows Best* by Kathy Henderson (Picture Corgi); range of items that feature in the book, such as a set of keys, a bath plug, a photo of a baby, a bowl of cooked spaghetti, a teddy; a tray; a piece of material; a bright box.

What's that sound?

Sharing the game

● Take the small bright box and place all of the items inside, or place them on the tray.
● Look at the book with your child. As you read the pages, offer each item for her to explore and make sounds with, demonstrating if necessary.
● Next, let her explore the items freely. Read the page or repeat the line in the book which refers to the item as she explores it.
● Read the rhyming pages slowly a few times over if her attention remains on one item for a while.
● At the end of the book look again at the items and name them, asking her to show you the keys, the photo and so on.
● Use the material to cover the items and then shake them or manipulate them in some way under the cover to create a sound. Invite her to guess which item is making the sound.

Taking it further

● Choose another similar book, which has pictures of objects you have around the home. Look at the book and then, with your child, gather some of the items to match with the illustrations or photographs.

● Play some matching games, such as placing a cup and saucer together, a toothbrush and toothpaste, soap and a flannel, a shoe and a sock and so on. Challenge your child to create pairs by matching.

STORY TIME

AGE RANGE
2-3 years

LEARNING OPPORTUNITIES
● To relate pictures and illustrations to real items
● To develop the sense of taste.

YOU WILL NEED
A book which involves food such as *Don't Put Your Finger In The Jelly Nelly!* by Nick Sharratt (Hippo); real food such as jelly; chocolate milk; a doughnut; spaghetti; strawberry jam; a child's knife; a biscuit or piece of bread.

Pudding play

Sharing the game
● After lunch or dinner sit down with your child to enjoy a book about food together.
● If you are using the book suggested above, then encourage him to participate by naming the foods he sees on the pages.
● Read it through again. This time, choose one or two of the foods in the book and put it on the table as you come to it in the story. You will need to make sure that you limit the number of tastings he makes, so as not to make him ill!
● Encourage him to point to one of the items on the table by asking him what he would like to taste.

● Mime some of the eating and tasting actions for your child's enjoyment. For example, pretend you are drinking the chocolate milk; pretend the jelly is wobbling on your spoon and pretend you are biting a doughnut!
● Read the book again and challenge him to remember the food that appeared next in the story.
● Talk about the different foods, discussing what you like and don't like.
● Finally let your child enjoy some of the foods! Encourage him to pour the milk himself, use a child's knife to cut the doughnut into small pieces before eating it, and spread the jam on a biscuit or piece of bread. Help and support him if he needs it and praise all his attempts.

Taking it further
● Cut pictures and photographs of food from magazines, look at them together.

STORY TIME

AGE RANGE
2-3 years

LEARNING OPPORTUNITIES
● To develop a sense of texture
● To develop vocabulary
● To encourage thinking skills.

YOU WILL NEED
A book of rhymes, such as *Twinkle, Twinkle Little Star* (Ladybird); a few plastic fish (bath toys would be ideal); some feathers; wool; cotton wool; a plate; a soft toy cat; a plate of cherries (or items from the rhymes in your chosen book); a tray; a piece of fabric.

Twinkle and shine

Sharing the game
● Gather the variety of items that are in the rhymes in your chosen book.
● Sit together and as she turns the pages, read the rhymes on each page. When you come to a rhyme for which you have a matching object, let her explore the items with you. Talk about the texture and colour of the objects and also draw her attention to the shape, size and weight of them.

● At the end of the rhyme, place the explored items onto the tray.
● Continue to do this until all the items are on the tray.
● Place the piece of fabric over the top of all the items.
● Read the rhymes again, and as you look at each page, challenge her to find the appropriate items from the tray. Do this first by touch, under the fabric, then by sight as she withdraws the item to see if she was correct.
● Once finished let her play freely with all of the items. Taste the cherries together, but ensure you have removed all the stones.

Taking it further
● Hide all the items in a basket under a tea towel, As you read the book, let her feel for the item.
● Place three of the items under small bowls. Challenge her to guess where the wool is, the cherries are and so on.

STORY TIME

LEARNING OPPORTUNITIES
● To encourage interaction
● To develop visual awareness
● To stimulate thinking.

YOU WILL NEED
A textured book which encourages your child to interact with the pages, such as That's Not My Tractor (*Touch-feely Board Books* series, Usborne Books); some toy cars, tractors and vehicles.

Texture books

Sharing the game
● Offer your child the textured book to explore. Encourage him to talk about what he sees as he looks at the pages.
● Read the book to him and encourage him to join in with the refrain, 'That's not my tractor…'.
● After reading the book several times, substitute some wrong words as you read it again. For example, say 'It's too rough', instead of 'It's too smooth'. Does your child spot the deliberate error? Don't worry if he doesn't, just correct yourself and try again. This time he may be anticipating your 'joke'!
● Now let your child play freely with the toy vehicles.
● Together, make a set of cars, a set of tractors and a set of trains.
● Choose a set and imitate the sequence of the book as you play. For example, you might say, 'That's not my train, it's buffers are too slippery!'.
● Encourage your child to join in by adding some suggestions of his own.

Taking it further
● Read some other books from the same series.
● Use the describing words to describe other objects around the house, such as a shiny tap, a soft carpet and a smooth bath.

Use these recipes to make a selection of malleable materials to tempt the senses.

Chocolate dough

Mix together 1½ cups of flour, ½ cup of drinking chocolate powder, ½ cup of salt, ½ tablespoon of cream of tartar, 1½ tablespoons of cooking oil and 1 cup of hot water.

When mixed, draw your child's attention to the smell of the chocolate. Instead of chocolate powder try adding scented chocolate powder, such as mint or orange. Challenge your child to identify the scents.

Fruit dough

Mix together 1 packet of fruit flavoured jelly crystals (approximately 25g), 2 cups of flour, 1 cup of salt, 4 tablespoons of cream of tartar, 2 cups of boiling water and 2 tablespoons of cooking oil.

Use this dough alongside some real fruit, reflective of the scent you used. Encourage your child to smell the dough and then cut the real fruit to compare.

THINK FIRST!
Take care to keep children away from the boiling water.

Play dough

Mix 4 cups of flour and 2 cups of salt. Add 4 tablespoons of oil. Gradually add 1 cup of water, stirring at first with a wooden spoon and then kneading with your hands.

If the dough is too stiff, add more water. If the dough is too sticky, add more flour.

Textured dough

Mix together 1 cup of flour, 1 cup of water, 2 cups of oatmeal, some herbs, sugar, sand and rice.

Let your child identify the various ingredients before they are added. Encourage him to feel the textures before and after each ingredient is added.

Soap dough

Mix together 2 cups of flour, ½ cup of salt, 2 tablespoons of poster paint, 1 tablespoon of liquid soap and ½ cup of water.

Make three quantities of this soap dough, using different soap scents in each one. Let your child help as much as possible.

Pudding paint

Mix together 5 cups of water, 2 cups of plain flour, half a cup of sugar and 3 tablespoons of salt. Pour all the ingredients into a saucepan and cook for about seven minutes over a medium heat – until the mixture is thick and bubbling. Allow the mixture to cool.

The mixture can be stored in an airtight container for up to two weeks. Add colouring and aromas as you wish.

Scented dough

Mix together 2 cups of flour, 1 cup of salt, 2 tablespoons of cooking oil, some scented ingredients (such as grated soap, peppermint or vanilla flavouring, cinnamon or tea leaves) and 1 cup of hot water.

Create a range of scented doughs by using a wide selection of aromas. Let your child choose which aroma he would like to add.

Share these rhymes with your child and enjoy making up some movements together as you say them.

Pat-a-cake, Pat-a-cake

Pat-a-cake, pat-a-cake, baker's man,
Bake me a cake as fast as you can.
Pat it and prick it, and mark it with B,
And put it in the oven for baby and me.

Traditional

Twinkling stars

Who made (the twinkling stars), (x3)?
Who made the twinkling stars? In the dark blue sky?
(Flash fingers above head.)

Who made (the flowers that grow), (x3)?
Who made the flowers that grow? In the long green grass.
(Bend and pretend to grow.)

Who made (the birds that fly), (x3)?
Who made the birds that fly? In the bright blue sky
(Flap arms like wings.)

Who made both (you and me), (x3)?
Who made both you and me. Who made all of us?
(Point away and to self.)

Who made the twinkling stars, the flowers that grow, the birds that fly?
Who made both you and me? Every little thing!
(Repeat all the actions.)

Traditional

Humpty Dumpty

Humpty Dumpty
sat on the wall,
Humpty Dumpty
had a great fall.
All the King's horses and
all the King's men,
Couldn't put Humpty
together again!

Traditional

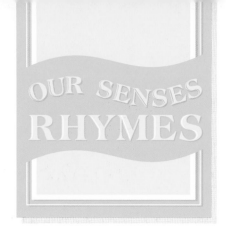

OUR SENSES RHYMES

Incy, Wincy Spider

Incy, wincy spider climbed up the water spout.
Down came the rain and washed poor Incy out!
Out came the sunshine and dried up all the rain,
So Incy, wincy spider climbed up the spout again!

Traditional

Sight

Open your eyes what do you see?
I can see you, you can see me.

Close them tight one, two, three,
I can't see you – you can't see me!

Two little eyes to open wide,
Watch and see, peep and hide.

Look all around, what do you see?
I can see you – can you see me?

Alice Sharp

Smell

Smell the flowers,
Smell the grass,
Smell the trees,
As you move past!

Smell the custard,
Smell the cake,
Smell the bread
As it is baked.

Alice Sharp

Hearing

Listen closely, what do you hear?
A laugh and a giggle,
A shout and a cheer.

Can you hear me whisper your name?
My little Becca, join in the game.

Alice Sharp

Round and Round the Garden

Round and round the garden,
Like a teddy bear,
One step,
Two steps,
Tickly under there.

Traditional